10372

Influential First Ladies

Other Books in the History Makers Series:

*History*MAKERS

Influential
First Ladies

By Sherri Peel Taylor

Lucent Books
P.O. Box 289011, San Diego, CA 92198-9011

On Cover: Center: Eleanor Roosevelt and Franklin D. Roosevelt
Top Right: Sarah Polk
Bottom Right: Hilary Rodham Clinton
Bottom Left: Jacqueline Kennedy
Top Left: Barbara Bush

Library of Congress Cataloging-in-Publication Data

Taylor, Sherri Peel.
    Influential first ladies / by Sherri Peel Taylor.
        p.   cm. — (History makers)
    Includes bibliographical references and index.
    Summary: Profiles the lives and work of America's most influential
First Ladies including: Sarah Childress Polk, Eleanor Roosevelt
Roosevelt, Barbara Pierce Bush, Hillary Rodham Clinton, Betty Bloomer
Ford, and Jacqueline Bouvier Kennedy.
    ISBN 1-56006-740-3 (alk. paper)
    1. Presidents' spouses—United States—Biography—Juvenile literature.
[1. First ladies. 2. Women—Biography.] I. Title. II. Series.
E176.2.P44   2001
973'.09'9—dc21   00-009684

Copyright 2001 by Lucent Books, Inc.
P.O. Box 289011, San Diego, California 92198-9011

Printed in the U.S.A.

CONTENTS

FOREWORD

The literary form most often referred to as "multiple biography" was perfected in the first century A.D. by Plutarch, a perceptive and talented moralist and historian who hailed from the small town of Chaeronea in central Greece. His most famous work, *Parallel Lives*, consists of a long series of biographies of noteworthy ancient Greek and Roman statesmen and military leaders. Frequently, Plutarch compares a famous Greek to a famous Roman, pointing out similarities in personality and achievements. These expertly constructed and very readable tracts provided later historians and others, including playwrights like Shakespeare, with priceless information about prominent ancient personages and also inspired new generations of writers to tackle the multiple biography genre.

The Lucent History Makers series proudly carries on the venerable tradition handed down from Plutarch. Each volume in the series consists of a set of six to eight biographies of important and influential historical figures who were linked together by a common factor. In *Rulers of Ancient Rome*, for example, all the figures were generals, consuls, or emperors of either the Roman Republic or Empire; while the subjects of *Fighters Against American Slavery*, though they lived in different places and times, all shared the same goal, namely the eradication of human servitude. Mindful that politicians and military leaders are not (and never have been) the only people who shape the course of history, the editors of the series have also included representatives from a wide range of endeavors, including scientists, artists, writers, philosophers, religious leaders, and sports figures.

Each book is intended to give a range of figures—some well known, others less known; some who made a great impact on history, others who made only a small impact. For instance, by making Columbus's initial voyage possible, Spain's Queen Isabella I, featured in *Women Leaders of Nations*, helped to open up the New World to exploration and exploitation by the European powers. Unarguably, therefore, she made a major contribution to a series of events that had momentous consequences for the entire world. By contrast, Catherine II, the eighteenth-century Russian queen, and Golda Meir, the modern Israeli prime minister, did not play roles of global impact; however, their policies and actions significantly influenced the historical development of both their own countries and their regional neighbors. Regardless of their relative importance in the greater historical scheme, all of the figures chronicled in the History Makers series made contributions to posterity; and their public achievements, as well as what is known about their private lives, are presented and evaluated in light of the most recent scholarship.

In addition, each volume in the series is documented and substantiated by a wide array of primary and secondary source quotations. The primary source quotes enliven the text by presenting eyewitness views of the times and culture in which each history maker lived; while the secondary source quotes, taken from the works of respected modern scholars, offer expert elaboration and/or critical commentary. Each quote is footnoted, demonstrating to the reader exactly where biographers find their information. The footnotes also provide the reader with the means of conducting additional research. Finally, to further guide and illuminate readers, each volume in the series features photographs, two bibliographies, and a comprehensive index.

The History Makers series provides both students engaged in research and more casual readers with informative, enlightening, and entertaining overviews of individuals from a variety of circumstances, professions, and backgrounds. No doubt all of them, whether loved or hated, benevolent or cruel, constructive or destructive, will remain endlessly fascinating to each new generation seeking to identify the forces that shaped their world.

A Changing Role

Many of America's first ladies are largely unknown to the general public. Names like Eliza Johnson (wife of the seventeenth president, Andrew Johnson) and Grace Coolidge (wife of the thirtieth president, Calvin Coolidge) are probably not recognizable to the average American. Others, however, have left their mark—on the position of first lady and sometimes, also, on history. Although never elected to office, many of these women have loyally served alongside their husbands and worked hard to improve the lives of the American people.

Yet since 1789 when George Washington took office as the first president and his wife began serving as his hostess, the role of first lady has often been a thankless job. No bands play stirring music when the first lady enters a room, and no constitutional amendments outline her duties. The women who have lived in the White House have been forced to feel their way along carefully, often guided by public opinion. One historian said, "The First Lady has no Constitutional or statutory duties at all, but she's almost constantly on display, and held to the ephemeral [fleeting] ideals of the moment. She's expected to be well-groomed, well-behaved and make bland statements on behalf of unexceptional causes."[1]

Therefore it is impossible to categorize first ladies as if the same thing were expected of each one. They lived at different times in history when demands on them varied widely and when a woman's role in the home, workplace, or White House meant something very different than it does today.

However, whatever their role, whether they charged to the forefront of American politics or chose to maintain a low profile, first ladies have all had similar obstacles to surmount. Every move they made was scrutinized, discussed, and publicized. Each faced a dizzying array of receptions, dinners, and parties. Yet even with all that the first ladies accomplished, the nation couldn't decide what to call them.

What's in a Name?

While the Congress debated about calling the president "His High Mightiness" or "His Patriotic Majesty," the first president's wife, Martha Washington, was called Lady Washington until some complained that it sounded like royalty. Other titles that were rejected included "Mrs. President" and "Presidentress"—Julia Tyler (wife of President John Tyler) called herself Mrs. President Tyler. No title fit the position or held public favor until 1849, when President Zachary Taylor called Dolley Madison "our First Lady"[2] during his eulogy of her. In 1860, a magazine used the term to describe unmarried

President James Madison's wife, Dolley, was the first to be called "First Lady."

President James Buchanan's niece and hostess. And in 1861, Mary Todd Lincoln was called the first lady by the *New York Herald* and the *Sacramento Union* newspapers. Finally, the presidents' wives had a title. Their job, however, was still developing.

A Changing Role

When Martha Washington was first lady, her major concerns were hosting the guests who came to visit her husband. She hosted receptions in her home each Friday, formal dinner parties every Thursday, and formal state gatherings twice a month. And because the number of people involved in politics at that time was small, she still found time to pay regular visits to congressmen's wives.

As the nation grew, however, so did the demands on the first lady—and the criticism of her work, particularly by the news media. The women's privacy was invaded in a way few other Americans had ever experienced. Any mistake they made was broadcast far and wide. Frances Cleveland and Jackie Kennedy were perhaps the most besieged by the press, and both fought to maintain their privacy. But no first lady has been as successful as Bess Truman at excluding the press from her life.

Changes in the times and attitudes of the public also affected the way Americans viewed first ladies. When Mary Todd Lincoln suffered from severe depression, for example, she was despised and criticized by those who had no understanding of the disease. A century later, however, Betty Ford spoke openly about her experience with depression. She never hid the fact that she had been treated by a psychiatrist or had taken tranquilizing medications. When Ida McKinley suffered epileptic seizures, her husband simply threw a handkerchief across her face to prevent the public from seeing the contortions of her face. More recently, Betty Ford and Nancy Reagan underwent life-saving surgery when it was discovered they had breast cancer, a disease that would have been fatal a century ago. Both spoke candidly about their experience.

Today it is not only accepted but expected that a first lady will take on a cause and pursue it to the best of her abilities, demanding public attention and asking for funds with which to carry out her objective. Americans want their first ladies to be intelligent and gracious leaders who set an example for the country and the world.

Affecting Change

Although women in the White House have often been diligent, ambitious, and loyal, a few have also been powerful and, at the

Mary Todd Lincoln suffered from depression and was criticized by the public because of it.

same time, individualists. Sarah Childress Polk, for instance, didn't feel obligated to follow in the footsteps of the genteel women who preceded her. Instead, she discreetly served as her husband's partner in politics. More than one hundred years later, Hillary Rodham Clinton took on a similar role, although hers was not discreet; her husband openly declared that she was his political partner. On the other hand, Jacqueline Bouvier Kennedy never made a display of the power she wielded while serving as her husband's translator and trusted adviser.

Betty Bloomer Ford publicly urged her husband to take women into his administration and act on policy giving them equal rights. She firmly maintained her position, doing whatever she could to gain support for the ideas she believed in. Barbara Bush, while in every way a partner to her husband, chose to focus on her family ties. And Eleanor Roosevelt enjoyed serving as her husband's eyes and ears to the world. She traveled widely, bringing back reports that FDR could use as a basis for his policy, decisions, and judgments.

In different ways, some of these first ladies made their roles powerful. Some influenced style worldwide. Others stood beside their husbands as policy advisers. Of the thirty-nine who have served as first lady, these six—Sarah Childress Polk, Eleanor Roosevelt Roosevelt, Jacqueline Bouvier Kennedy, Betty Bloomer Ford, Barbara Pierce Bush, and Hillary Rodham Clinton—stand out for the pivotal role they played in redefining the position and image of first lady.

CHAPTER 1

Sarah Childress Polk: Adviser to a President

Ambitious, intelligent, and a religious zealot, Sarah Childress Polk never doubted her goals in life. She was consumed by a love of politics. When James K. Polk asked for her hand in marriage, she insisted he run for political office. Later he said he believed that "had he remained the clerk of the legislature she would never have married him."[3]

Sarah was an impressive first lady. She was well educated and a formidable opponent in any debate. At White House receptions, instead of remaining with the ladies in the sitting room as was expected, she preferred the company of male visitors who were sure to be discussing politics.

Acknowledged by all as a serious politician when few women were, Sarah Polk served as her husband's primary and sometimes only adviser. He often said of her advice, "None but Sarah, knew so intimately my private affairs."[4] She was the first woman to openly serve as her husband's partner politically.

Her beliefs that God had already decided the course of everyone's life and that, on orders from God, the United States should include the entire North American continent were large factors in her husband's policy making. Such beliefs led her to the conclusion that whatever means she and her husband took to attain their aims, it was all really in the pursuit of what God wanted. Sarah once said, "I recognize nothing in myself; I am only an atom in the hands of God."[5]

Growing Up

Sarah Childress was born on September 4, 1803, near Murfreesboro, Tennessee, to a wealthy planter named Captain Joel Childress and his wife, Elizabeth Whitsitt Childress. Captain Childress was often visited by Andrew Jackson (who ultimately became president), and Sarah was allowed to listen in on their political conversations, an experience that fostered her interest in politics.

Well educated and ambitious, Sarah Polk took an active role in the politics of her husband's presidency.

Captain Childress believed that his daughter should be educated just as his sons were, and although Sarah was not allowed to attend the all-male school her brothers did, their teacher came to the house and taught her in the evenings. Later she attended the most prestigious women's academy of her day, the Moravian College. This college was operated by a religious group that placed great emphasis on moral conduct. There, Sarah took on the characteristics of an extremely religious person: an absolute faith in God (believing especially that she had been chosen to succeed) and a steadfast commitment to attend church every week.

Sarah paid a lot of attention to her dress, which was always perfect. Careful grooming not only gave her extra confidence, it gave a good impression to those with whom she wished to associate. A visitor once said she "is a very handsome woman. Her hair is very black, her dark eyes and complexion remind one of the Spanish donnas [ladies]. She is well read, and has much talent for conversation and is very popular."[6] It was her habit to style her hair carefully, arranging it in long ringlets.

Sarah's exceptionally sharp mind, gracious manners, and talent for conversation did not escape the notice of some important people. One of those people was James Polk, a Tennessee politician. Polk was impressed with Sarah's wit and intelligence. The two met in 1821, soon after Sarah graduated from college, and quickly began a relationship. When Polk asked her to marry him in 1823, she agreed, but on one condition: that he run for a seat on the Tennessee legislature. Sarah was certain that she wanted a life centered around politics, but since she could not run for office herself, she insisted that any man she married had to do so.

Although he was a serious and hardworking member of the Democratic Party, Polk wasn't sure he'd be a successful candidate. However, with Sarah's urging, he decided to run for a seat in the Tennessee state legislature. Following his win, James and Sarah were married on January 1, 1824, when she was twenty and he was twenty-nine.

The newly married Polks moved into a small two-room log house, which suited Sarah perfectly. The tiny home placed no heavy demands on Sarah, who had no interest in household chores. She felt she had much more important things to do, including encouraging her husband's political goals and building a circle of friends who might someday support her husband's political aspirations.

Even though their marriage was essentially a happy one, the Polks never had any children. History is silent as to why, but certainly Sarah was not saddened by this. Not having children meant she was not tied to her home, a fact that left her free to travel with Polk to the state capital when the legislature convened.

During these years, Sarah and her husband formed a very close relationship and learned that they actually complemented each other well. For instance, although James was a hard worker, he did not care to read. Sarah, on the other hand, did, and it was her avid desire to learn that kept him current on state affairs.

Progress in Politics

In November 1824, during their first year of marriage, James Polk was elected to the U.S. House of Representatives, and Sarah was excited to move to Washington, D.C. The city was the center of all things political, where the most powerful men lived and worked, an ideal situation for a woman who loved the political arena.

In Washington, Sarah arranged small dinner parties and intimate gatherings of Democratic and city leaders. She also managed to befriend many important men in government. Her greatest pleasure was joining these politicians for discussions of the issues of the day, including the problem of whether new states admitted into the Union should be allowed to practice slavery. Sarah was careful always to preface her opinions with "Mr. Polk said" or "Mr. Polk believes." This allowed those she spoke with to pretend that she was simply parroting her husband's ideas, even when they knew better. She would most certainly have drawn great criticism had she attempted to voice her own thoughts as if they were equal to the men's. In 1825 women were not expected to have opinions other than those of their husbands, but Sarah was able to overcome these objections by using caution and self-control while she spoke with the men.

Furthermore, it was never Sarah's wish to undermine her husband's position. Instead, she remained his partner at all times and depended on him for any political prominence of her own. Rather than her political aspirations being an attempt to defy her husband, or make herself seem more intelligent or shrewd, her aim was to build a supportive group of politicians who could keep her and her husband informed of popular opinion and back Polk in any potential bid for public office.

Sarah not only understood the social side of politics, but was also an expert on political strategy. She knew that the relationships she and her husband made could prove a decisive force in later years. Once such relationship was with Andrew Jackson. One of Polk's earliest political counselors and an old family friend of Sarah's, Jackson served as president of the United States from 1829 to 1837. Polk's association with Jackson helped secure him a leadership position in the U.S. House of Representatives. Polk was ultimately elected as the Speaker of the House, the representative who led the decision-making process and the majority party. It was a position he held for two terms, and Sarah was very proud of her husband's accomplishments.

At the end of Polk's second term as Speaker of the House, the Democratic Party, with the powerful former president Jackson as its leader, convinced Polk to run for governor of Tennessee. Sarah wholeheartedly supported this move. She saw it as a clever political decision because she was well aware that Polk's options in the House were limited.

When Polk ran for governor of Tennessee in 1839, Sarah acted as his campaign manager, which was unheard of at that time. She arranged his speaking schedule and handled his mail. Most of this she did from her home, and did not actually travel with Polk during the campaign. She diligently arranged receptions and dinners, events aimed at gathering strength and support for Polk's political career. A gracious and intelligent hostess, Sarah filled her guest lists with political leaders in an attempt to build a solid base for her husband's career.

Although her hostessing impressed many people in the Tennessee governor's mansion, her husband did not have a similar effect on the voters. After one lackluster two-year term as governor, he was not reelected. Two more failed attempts to regain the office seemed to signal the end of James Polk's political career.

At first Sarah's faith in herself was shaken. She strongly believed that she and her husband had been chosen by God to attain higher office. That belief had only been bolstered by Polk's success in Washington. Failure did not fit into her vision of what God

Former president Andrew Jackson was instrumental in James Polk's being elected president.

had in store for them. Yet despite the setbacks, Sarah remained determined to get back into politics. The opportunity came in 1844 when Andrew Jackson summoned Polk to his home near Nashville, Tennessee, for an important political conference.

A Presidential Candidate

Still a powerful figure in politics, former president Jackson had decided that the party could not support Martin Van Buren, a former Democratic president who was once again seeking the presidency. Van Buren had lost a second bid for president in 1840 but seemed like a viable candidate in 1844. However, slavery and expanding U.S. territory were not issues in 1844. Van Buren's refusal to admit the newly acquired Texas territory into the Union infuriated Jackson. As a result, Jackson vowed to keep Van Buren from gaining the party's nomination. Instead, he decided, James Polk should run as the Democrats' candidate, and Jackson called a conference to name his choice.

Those at the conference must have been surprised when Jackson chose Polk, a relatively minor politician, as their candidate for the coming election, but the former president had good reason to support Polk. Shrewd politician that he was, Jackson saw slavery as the campaign's major issue, and he theorized that only an unknown candidate whose views on slavery were not general knowledge could win the election. Northerners who might vote for James Polk would not know he was pro-slavery (even though, by

Martin Van Buren, former democratic president, lost the party's nomination to James Polk in 1844.

this time, the Polks owned a plantation operated by slaves). Although there was adequate newspaper and magazine coverage of events nationwide, it was slow and most often local in nature. Therefore, it could be weeks or months before Polk's pro-slavery leanings would be uncovered. By that time, Jackson was certain, James Polk would be established in the White House.

Jackson's theories proved well founded when, in the fall of 1844, Polk was elected president. Finally, Sarah's beliefs in her own destiny and her husband's had come true.

In the White House

James Polk's administration was greatly affected by his wife and her strict religious beliefs. Sarah banned dancing, drinking alcoholic beverages, and card playing in the White House, reasoning that "To dance in these rooms [the White House] would be undignified and it would be respectful neither to the house nor to the office. How indecorous it would seem for dancing to be going on in one apartment while in another we were conversing with dignitaries of the republic or ministers of the gospel. This unseemly juxtaposition would be likely to occur at any time were such an amusement permitted."[7]

Despite her stringent rules against dancing and card playing, Sarah loved giving and attending dazzling parties and wearing beautiful gowns. At one time it was reported that she spent $600 for dresses from France, a sum considered a fortune in those days.

Although a few people criticized her strict rules, many praised Sarah for her religious convictions and wrote to commend and encourage her. Some hoped the nation as a whole would benefit. Others thought the new attitude in Washington would suit the importance of the work being done there.

The *Nashville Union* wrote of Sarah Polk, "All will agree that by the exclusion of frivolities and her excellent deportment [behavior] in other respects she has conferred [given] additional dignity on the executive department of her government."[8]

Sarah's religion also demanded strict observance of the Sabbath. That meant on Sunday, neither she nor her husband could do any work at all. When she refused to allow her husband to receive dignitaries from other countries or conduct important government business on Sunday, however, some people felt she had overstepped her bounds. Government officials complained. One who wrote of this later said,

President James Polk, in office from 1845 to 1849, was pro-slavery.

> Public comment became more pronounced until her attitude was discussed from every angle, and the consensus of general opinion was to the effect that her private religious views were wholly personal and should not be intruded into national affairs nor should established national functions either be curtailed or modified to conform to them.[9]

Slaves in the White House

Sarah was just as rigid about the Polk family finances as she was about religion. What fortunes she and her husband had built, she had every intention of preserving. In order to cut costs at the

White House, one of her first actions was to replace servants with slaves because servants who worked in the White House had to be paid; slaves did not. The basement of the White House was re-arranged into sleeping quarters for the Polks' slaves.

Sarah believed that slavery was a just and acceptable institution. One day while watching several of the slaves work outside, she said to her husband, "The writers of the Declaration of Independence were mistaken when they affirmed that all men are created equal. There are those men toiling in the sun while you are writing, and I am sitting here fanning myself, in this house as airy and delightful as a palace, surrounded by every comfort. These men did not choose such a lot in life, neither did we ask for ours; we are created for these places."[10] Clearly, Sarah Polk thought she and her husband were superior, not just because of their own personal qualities but because she believed they had been chosen to fill a special place in life. It was this idea, that she was special, selected by God, that influenced Sarah Polk's outlook on everything.

Conversations with the First Lady

Politicians who had the privilege to speak with Sarah acknowledged that she was an entertaining conversationalist. Senator Charles Sumner, who was a critic of President Polk, said that her warm manner won him over when her husband could not. Franklin Pierce, who later became the fourteenth president, also admitted to finding enormous pleasure in his and Sarah's conversations. And many people said that Sarah enjoyed the subject of politics so much that she often talked through rather than ate dinner and hosts were forced to reheat her meal for her.

Not everyone supported Sarah, however, and there were those whose criticisms she could not forgive. Congressman John Van Buren, son of former president Martin Van Buren, for example, denounced nearly every move of the Polk presidency, and Sarah banned him from the White House. Her husband then attempted a reconciliation by inviting the young man to a reception without telling Sarah. When she discovered Van Buren had been invited, Sarah tore up his invitation and made certain he did not attend.

Just as Polk supported Sarah in her ban of John Van Buren, he also did not argue with her policies when some of his cabinet members complained about Sarah's stringent rules on entertaining. Rather than order his wife to relax her principles, Polk conceded that entertaining was under Sarah's jurisdiction, not his. He considered such things minor matters, and said his major concern

Believing that slavery was an acceptable institution, President and Mrs. Polk replaced White House servants with slaves.

was the addition of more territory to the continental United States, a policy that the Polks called their Manifest Destiny.

Manifest Destiny

The theme of the Polk years was Manifest Destiny, which expressed the idea that America had been chosen by God as superior to all other nations and was predestined to include the entire continent from the Atlantic to the Pacific coast. It was a theory that went hand in hand with Sarah's own belief system and would serve to boost James Polk's confidence in the face of many difficulties. Some historians claim that the president stood firm under pressure because of his belief that the future had already been decided. Thus, he could do no wrong, and only had to wait for things to work out.

During Polk's administration, the United States did expand to the Pacific coast. He brought more land area under the control of his government than any other president since Thomas Jefferson.

War with Mexico

The first big success of Polk's presidency was the addition of Texas to the United States. It wasn't an acquisition that came easily, though. In fact, it required that the United States fight a war with Mexico over the southern boundary line. Polk believed the Rio Grande formed a natural border between the United States and Mexico. The Mexican government, however, did not agree. As a result, Polk decided to provoke a war with Mexico to force the issue. He ordered General Winfield Scott and General Zachary Taylor to Texas to stake out the Rio Grande. General Taylor's orders were to stand as a challenge to any forces that might attempt to cross the river. Taylor's men also taunted the Mexican soldiers across the river in an attempt to force a fight. When one Mexican general could bear the harassment no longer, he crossed the river with his troops and a small skirmish resulted. Polk used this incident as grounds to declare war on Mexico.

In reality, it wasn't much of a war. The Mexican government was bankrupt and fell easily. Supply lines broke down and left Mexico's soldiers without food or proper clothing. Furthermore, the men had not been paid in months and had lost all will to fight. At the end of the war, Mexico gave the United States more than half a million square miles of territory.

For the Polks, it was a tremendous victory. Of the situation, Sarah said, "I regard the results following the Mexican war, that is, the adding of California and New Mexico to the territory of the United States, as among the most important events in the history

President Polk declared war on Mexico in 1846 over the southern border of Texas.

Mrs. Polk (seated) died at the age of eighty-seven, outliving her husband by forty-two years.

of this country. Of course there were some opposed to it; there is always someone opposed to everything."[11] The opponents, however, were few and were not particularly vocal, and the Polks simply ignored them.

Advising the President

During the war with Mexico and throughout James Polk's presidency, his wife remained his most trusted adviser. In fact, the president so relied on his wife's advice that he never assembled a cabinet, the small band of advisers usually essential to a president's policy-making decisions. Polk wrote in his diary about his cabinet: "I have conducted the government without their aid. It is only occasionally that a great measure or new question arises upon which I need the . . . advice of my Cabinet."[12] He went on to point to Sarah as his only confidant.

Sarah's opinion mattered a great deal to her husband and to others. Even the opposing party praised her. Henry Clay, the candidate whom Polk defeated in the 1844 election, said that he had heard a lot of criticism of Polk's administration but that "All agree in commending . . . [Sarah's] excellent administration."[13]

Despite her many admirers, there were people who didn't approve of the influence Sarah had over her husband. One in particular, Vice President George M. Dallas, disliked her tremendously and accused her of taking over his job.

Leaving Washington

Sarah believed her husband should try for a second term in office, but he was not a popular president and chose not to run. Also, Polk's health had always been fragile, in spite of which he'd always pushed himself to the limits of his endurance. The couple left Washington in 1849 after the inauguration of President Zachary Taylor. They intended to take a long trip that Sarah hoped would improve Polk's health, but he soon became very ill and died three months after they left office.

After her husband's death, Sarah returned to their home in Nashville and spent the remainder of her life building a museum to their years in the White House. She died August 14, 1891, at the age of eighty-seven and was buried beside her husband in Nashville, Tennessee.

Eleanor Roosevelt Roosevelt: First Lady of the World

When Eleanor Roosevelt died in 1962, former president Harry Truman stated: "I told her she was First Lady of the World."[14] Few would dispute the title. She had served as first lady of the United States for twelve years, from 1933 to 1945, working tirelessly to change laws, institute programs for the underprivileged, and overcome inequalities. From a timid and lonely orphan, Eleanor had developed into a passionate advocate for those less fortunate than herself.

Her most lasting tribute benefited not only her own country but the entire world. It was primarily through her extraordinary dedication and drive that the United Nations Universal Declaration of Human Rights was drafted, debated, and finally overwhelmingly approved. The declaration outlined the basic human rights to which every man, woman, and child on earth was entitled. Eleanor called it a wonderful charter to benefit all mankind and the crowning achievement of her public service. For the first time, an international document stated that people everywhere should have the same freedoms that Americans had long been enjoying in the United States.

In Her Youth

Anna Eleanor Roosevelt was born on October 11, 1884, in New York City, the oldest of three children. Her mother, Anna Hall Roosevelt, was a high-society beauty and her father, Elliot Roosevelt, was the brother of Theodore Roosevelt, the twenty-sixth president of the United States. Eleanor grew up wealthy and privileged but unhappy. Her father adored his oldest child, but he was addicted to pain medication and alcohol, and was seldom around. When he was home, however, Eleanor thrived on the time they

10372

Eleanor Roosevelt (right) with her father and brothers, Elliot (left) and Hall (center) circa 1890.

spent together. On the other hand, her mother was quick to point out the young girl's faults. From the day Eleanor was old enough to realize her mother considered her ugly, the child began to see herself as different. She became a bit of a recluse and had very few friends. Before she was ten years old, both her parents had died, her mother of diphtheria and her father after a debilitating fall. After their deaths, Eleanor and her brothers Ellie and Hall were sent to live with their Grandmother Hall in Manhattan.

Eleanor's grandmother imposed rigorous rules on her new charges. She was unwilling to tolerate any childlike behavior and raised the children in a strict, proper environment. There was no play room, and Eleanor had to practice walking perfectly straight by having a stick placed against her back. There was an attitude of gloom and silence that enveloped the entire household. As a result, Eleanor felt that she was not quite equal to her Roosevelt cousins and aunts and uncles, who enjoyed a less rigid lifestyle. Her mother's cruel remarks about her looks, her parents' early deaths, and her treatment while living with her grandmother affected Eleanor deeply. She grew up to be a quiet, solemn child who often daydreamed about her father, whom she missed terribly.

Before she died, Eleanor's mother had made it clear that she wanted Eleanor to be educated in Europe, so in September 1899,

Eleanor left for Allenswood, a school just outside London. There she began to make friends and gain confidence and poise. The headmistress, Marie Souvestre, was taken with the tall, solemn child and wrote to Grandmother Hall, "All that you said when she [Eleanor] came here of the purity of her heart, the nobleness of her thought have been verified by her conduct among people who were perfect strangers to her. . . . She is full of sympathy for all those who live with her and shows an intelligent interest in everything."[15] Eleanor became Souvestre's favorite student.

Love and Marriage

After three years at Allenswood, Eleanor returned to America, where she began to encounter her fifth cousin Franklin Delano Roosevelt at family gatherings, Christmas parties, and once while she was traveling by train. The young lawyer was fascinated by Eleanor and he sought her company, although Eleanor couldn't believe that he might truly be interested in her. He persisted, however, and convinced her of his sincerity, and they became engaged.

Eleanor (center, back row) attended Allenswood School where she gained confidence and poise.

Eleanor and Franklin Roosevelt were married on March 17, 1905, in New York City. After the wedding, the couple moved into a duplex, with his mother occupying one side and the newlyweds the other. There Eleanor and FDR settled into married life.

It was during those early years of marriage that the differences in Eleanor's and FDR's personalities became obvious. Because of her upbringing in a house where play was forbidden, Eleanor was sober and diligent, whereas her husband loved to have fun. She could never find it in herself to do that. "Duty," she once said, "was perhaps the motivating force of my life, often excluding

Eleanor married her cousin, Franklin Delano Roosevelt, in New York City in 1905.

what might have been joy or pleasure. I looked at everything from the point of view of what I ought to do, rarely from the point of view of what I wanted to do. . . . I was never carefree."[16]

This philosophy served her well when it came to making life decisions. For example, when FDR decided to enter the political field, she dutifully backed his decision and listened to all his plans with a great deal of interest. In 1910 FDR won his first elective office, a seat in the New York State Senate, and the young family, which now included three children, happily moved to the state capital of Albany.

Living in Public View

In Albany, Eleanor discovered that she would play a key role in her husband's career when the government dinners and receptions became her responsibility. She soon developed a deep interest in FDR's work, attended Senate debates, and discussed them later with her husband.

Outwardly, however, she was still unsure of herself. Eleanor saw her role as that of wife and mother. It would be quite some time before she felt comfortable as an assertive woman whose thoughts and beliefs counted for something. In fact, when FDR came out publicly in favor of giving women the right to vote, the idea shocked her. She had never even considered that she or other women had such rights. She said, "I had never given the matter serious thought, for I took it for granted that men were superior creatures and knew more about politics than women did."[17]

Life in Albany came to an end in 1912, when FDR was appointed assistant secretary of the navy, and the family moved to Washington, D.C. There, the Roosevelts' life revolved around visiting friends and colleagues and dining out night after night. Their social schedule became so heavy that Eleanor hired a young woman named Lucy Mercer to serve as social secretary. Miss Mercer became more than an employee; Eleanor often invited the young woman to dinner parties. And she began to think of Miss Mercer as a friend rather than an employee. However, as Miss Mercer's relationship with the Roosevelts progressed and the young woman became a regular visitor, often when Eleanor was away, Eleanor started to get suspicious.

A Changing Relationship

During this time, Eleanor's life revolved around her children Anna, Elliot, James, Franklin Jr., and John. The life she and FDR built together had taken the place of the family life she had never had as a child. This life was torn apart, however, when Eleanor began to suspect that Franklin and Lucy Mercer were having an affair. At first, Eleanor had only rumors as evidence. However, she soon found the concrete proof she'd been looking for.

In 1918 on a trip to Europe, FDR became gravely ill. When he arrived home in an ambulance, he was sent straight to bed with double pneumonia. With her husband so sick, Eleanor had to take care of all his mail. In doing so, she found love letters Miss Mercer had written to FDR. Eleanor's suspicions were confirmed.

The discovery that her husband was involved with a younger, prettier woman forced Eleanor to reevaluate her opinion of herself. It wasn't easy, and the incident forever changed her life. She was troubled with mood swings and feelings of depression as she sought to find her own place in a world without FDR as its center. In the end, though, the experience ultimately gave her the confidence to stand on her own. Later, Eleanor's friend Joseph Lash said, "[Eleanor] was a woman of sorrow who had surmounted her unhappiness and managed to carry on, stoical toward herself, understanding and tender toward others. She had turned her sorrow into a strengthening thing."[18]

Lucy Mercer's love affair with FDR continued until his death in 1945.

Eleanor offered to divorce FDR, and he considered it, saying he was in love with Miss Mercer. He didn't consider it for long, however, because his family was in an uproar over the matter. FDR's mother threatened to cut him out of his inheritance if he left Eleanor. His political backers were also in a frenzy. During the first half of the twentieth century, a man who had been divorced was not likely to be elected to any office, much less the presidency. Louis Howe, FDR's closest political adviser, explained that he had a choice to make: Miss Mercer or his career. It wasn't long before Franklin Roosevelt had to admit that leaving his wife and family would end his political life. For the sake of her five children,

Eleanor agreed to a reconciliation if her husband promised never to see Miss Mercer again.

In the wake of the Mercer affair, Eleanor and FDR continued their life together, but it changed forever. From that point on, their relationship became more of an agreeable partnership held together by a deep emotional tie. James, their son, said, "After that [the Mercer affair] father and mother had an armed truce that endured to the day he died. . . . There was always an affection between them."[19] Eleanor never knew that FDR continued seeing Miss Mercer, who was with him when he died many years later.

Eleanor said later that it was during those days that her interest in politics began to take shape. Where once she had been shocked by the idea of a woman voicing her opinion by voting, now she wanted to speak out for the rights of others. She joined the State of New York's Women's Democratic Party and rose to a leadership position. She learned to give speeches and traveled over the state to found other Democratic women's clubs. Her newfound courage and confidence would prove absolutely necessary four years later when her husband became seriously ill.

A Debilitating Illness

It was on a family trip to Campobello Island in New Brunswick, Canada, in the summer of 1921 that tragedy struck. FDR awoke with a high fever and stabbing pains in his back and legs. He was diagnosed with polio, a crippling disease with no cure. Doctors said he would never walk again, but Eleanor declared that her husband would never give up. She worked tirelessly to help him, sleeping on a small cot in his bedroom to be near him at night and serving as his nurse for months, bathing him, massaging him, and exercising his legs. She said, "In many ways, this was the most trying winter of my entire life."[20]

Eleanor tried never to look at FDR's disability as career ending. As she encouraged her husband's belief that he could walk again, she became more confident in herself. As she watched FDR progress from a wheelchair to crutches and then to leg braces, she noticed he had changed in other ways as well. "Franklin's illness was a blessing in disguise," she said, "for it gave him strength and courage he had not had before. He had to think out the fundamentals of living and learn the greatest of all lessons—infinite patience and never-ending persistence."[21]

For Eleanor, this illness added to her growing self-confidence. Yet again, crisis had contributed to a deepening and widening of her own character. She said that FDR's illness "made me stand on my own two feet in regard to my husband's life, my own life and my children's training," and without this, she might have remained "a completely colorless echo of my husband. . . . I might have stayed a weak character forever."[22]

First Lady to the Nation

In the early 1930s, an economic depression engulfed the United States, putting millions out of work. Franklin D. Roosevelt proposed a plan to put things back in order, and the American people believed in him. In 1932 Americans overwhelmingly elected FDR president of the United States.

This photo of FDR (left), visiting a Boy Scout Camp at Lake Kanohwahke, New York, is the last taken of him walking unassisted; two weeks later, he was diagnosed with polio.

As the president's wife, Eleanor feared losing the independence she had begun to cherish. She knew the White House was a difficult place for a woman. The many duties of being first lady would control her life. However, even as she despaired for herself, she was glad for her husband, saying,

> I was happy for [Franklin], because I knew in many ways it would make up for the blow that fate had dealt him when he was stricken with infantile paralysis [polio]; and I had implicit confidence in his ability to help the country in a crisis. . . . But for myself I was deeply troubled. As I saw it, this meant the end of any personal life of my own. I knew what traditionally should lie before me: I had watched Mrs. Theodore Roosevelt and had seen what it meant to be the wife of a president, and I cannot say that I was pleased at the prospect. . . . The turmoil in my heart and mind was rather great."[23]

Despite her reservations, Eleanor helped in every way possible to see that FDR's policies were put into action, and his need for Eleanor grew during his time in office. Bound to a wheelchair, FDR could not easily visit hospitals, prisons, or other institutions, so Eleanor became his legs as well as his eyes and ears. Where he couldn't walk, she traveled. What he couldn't see, she reported. He trusted Eleanor to report faithfully to him what he needed to know.

The nation first became aware of the role Eleanor played in her husband's administration when unemployed war veterans marched on Washington, D.C., in 1933 for the second time, asking for bonuses promised them. In 1932 during their first march, former president Herbert Hoover's administration used tear gas to disperse the veterans. The second time, however, Eleanor, acting as her husband's eyes and ears, visited the men. She said,

> Hesitatingly, I got out and walked over to where I saw a line-up of men waiting for food. . . . They looked at me curiously and one of them asked my name and what I wanted. When I said I just wanted to see how they were getting on, they asked me to join them.

She spent an hour talking with them about their problems. One of the veterans commented, "Hoover sent the army. Roosevelt sent his wife."[24]

Her courage in visiting the camp (the disgruntled men had been expecting a fight) made a deep impression on the veterans. They and the suffering country learned that the new first lady was going

Eleanor, Franklin, and their son, James, arrive at the White House after the 1933 inauguration ceremonies.

to be different, that she was willing to reach out to people. Eleanor, in turn, was heartened by the veterans' response. She became determined to do more.

In her quest to serve as Franklin's representative, she traveled nationwide visiting slums and mental institutions, prisons and hospitals. She delighted the nation when she donned a hard hat and went down into a mine in West Virginia. If the government instigated a relief program, Eleanor got the job of inspecting it. She said, "I think in some of us there is an urge to do certain things and, if we did not do them, we would feel that we were not fulfilling the job which we had been given opportunities and talents to do. . . . I am in a position where I can do the most good to help the most people."[25]

As Eleanor's confidence grew, she became more deeply involved in her husband's policies and programs. She pushed for equal pay for women, she persuaded officials to use surplus farm goods to feed the hungry, and she helped start a program that provided part-time jobs for young people who wanted to continue their education. Through it all, she maintained a daily newspaper column in which she wrote about everything she did in detail. The American people, in turn, became familiar with Eleanor and developed a personal attachment to her.

Final Years in the White House

When FDR was reelected in 1940, the first president elected to a third term, he promised to keep the nation out of the war raging in Europe. Because of her own travels and the people she had spoken with, Eleanor wasn't certain that was possible. She wrote in her column, "No one can honestly promise you today peace at home or abroad. All any human being can do is to promise that he will do his utmost to prevent this country being involved in war."[26]

In December 1941, Eleanor's instincts proved correct, and the United States entered World War II. Traditionally, U.S. presidents have visited soldiers during wartime. Since FDR could not make the morale-boosting trip, Eleanor went in his place. She traveled

Mrs. Roosevelt (seated, smiling) visiting with miners at Willow Grove mine in Clairsville, Ohio, in 1936.

to the South Pacific, ignoring the advice of officials who feared for her safety, and visited seventeen islands, including Guadalcanal, New Caledonia, and Efate. While on this tour, she toured hospital wards filled with young men horribly disfigured in battle. Later, Admiral William F. Halsey, who was in command of the U.S. forces in the South Pacific, said that Eleanor had accomplished more good among the troops than any other person during the war:

> [I] marveled at her hardihood, both physical and mental . . . she went into every ward, stopped at every bed and spoke to every patient: What was his name? How did he feel? Was there anything he needed? Could she take a message home for him? . . . [She] walked for miles, and she saw patients. . . . But I marveled most at their expressions as she leaned over them. It was a sight I will never forget.[27]

In 1944, FDR was reelected to a fourth term in office, but he was visibly weaker. Photographs of the time show that his face was thin and he had dark circles beneath his eyes. He was no longer able to attend long conferences and didn't have the strength to hear his wife's reports as he previously had. He also tired quickly.

Ignoring the advice of officials, Mrs. Roosevelt traveled throughout the South Pacific during World War II visiting American troops.

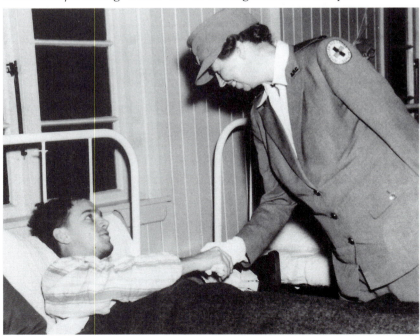

In an attempt to get some rest, he made a visit to Georgia's Warm Springs Resort in late March. On April 12, 1945, Eleanor received a call from Steve Early, FDR's advisor and press agent, requesting that she return immediately to Washington, D.C. "I did not even ask why. I knew in my heart that something dreadful had happened."[28]

She was right. FDR had died of a cerebral hemorrhage. With his death, Eleanor told her friends she felt the story of her life was over, but it certainly wasn't. Instead, the time had come for Eleanor to make a decision about her own future.

Delegate to the United Nations Assembly

In late 1945, Eleanor received a call from President Harry Truman, asking her to serve as one of five delegates to the United Nations Assembly in London. The assembly was an attempt to organize nations around the world to promote peace. Eleanor gladly accepted.

It was not going to be easy, however. Among the others chosen by Truman were a secretary of state, two senators, and the representative to the U.N. Security Council. Although Eleanor had been accepted on the delegation, the others were not eager to share their work with her, partly because they thought she lacked the necessary experience but also because she was a woman. They dismissed Eleanor as weak and emotional, ignoring her record of public service. At that time, few women had proven their abilities in public roles of responsibility, and the men appointed to serve with her doubted she was capable of handling a job that dealt with the problems facing the nations of the world. Without her knowledge, the men met and appointed her to an office they felt would be menial. She was assigned to Committee Three, which would deal with humanitarian, educational, and cultural questions; the rest of the delegation felt these would be noncontroversial issues. It wasn't long before they discovered their error.

Committee Three

Committee Three was in fact a hotbed of controversy. There were more than a million people displaced by the war in Europe, a problem that plagued the European nations. The question was whether evacuees should be sent to places chosen by the United Nations Assembly or return to their former homes. This issue fell into Eleanor's lap.

As the only delegate on that committee for the United States, it was up to Eleanor to represent the American view, that each person should be allowed to return home. Due mainly to Eleanor's influence, and her diligent argument that evacuees were entitled to return to their homes, the committee decided in favor of sending them back to their own countries. It was a victory for the American delegation and for Eleanor. The committee's decision proved to her detractors that Eleanor was indeed a powerful force in the effort to build a peacekeeping organization.

Declaration of Human Rights

In 1946 Eleanor was elected head of the United Nations Human Rights Commission. It was the commission's task to draft a document outlining the rights that every person, worldwide, should have. It would grant people the rights of speech, fair trials, and an education. It also sought to raise the standard of living. On December 10, 1948, the Universal Declaration of Human Rights was approved by the entire assembly. In an unprecedented move, everyone in attendance stood to honor Eleanor. Those who had worked with her at the assembly knew she had pushed her committee to its limits, often urging them to work late hours, in an attempt to create a declaration everyone could agree on.

In 1953, Eleanor resigned from her position at the U.N., but she continued to be an influence in politics nationwide. She spoke her

In 1947, Mrs. Roosevelt (second from left) attended an open meeting of the Second Session of the U.N. General Assembly in New York.

As head of the United Nations Human Rights Commission, Eleanor was instrumental in the creation of the Universal Declaration of Human Rights which was unanimously approved in 1948.

mind on civil rights, nuclear weapons, and any other issues that concerned her. When John F. Kennedy became president in 1961, he offered Eleanor another position as a U.N. delegate and appointed her to the advisory board of the Peace Corps. She accepted but was beginning to tire easily, saying, "For some time now my children and my friends have been warning me that I must slow down. I am willing to slow down but I just don't know how."[29]

It was a rare blood disease, aplastic anemia, that finally slowed Eleanor down and forced her to cut back on her activities. Although she kept her illness from the public, her friends and family knew she was very sick. As long as she was able, though, she carried on with her efforts to improve the lives of others. It was what made Eleanor happy. She said, "If anyone were to ask me what I want out of life, I would say the opportunity for doing something useful, for in no other way, I am convinced, can true happiness be attained."[30]

Eleanor Roosevelt died on November 7, 1962, of a stroke at age seventy-eight. Her mission as she saw it was always to place duty first, and she showed her commitment to that mission by working for the underprivileged, for equality for women, and for a peaceful future for the world. She had many successes and had done the very best she was able to do.

CHAPTER 3

Jacqueline Bouvier Kennedy: American Royalty

Around the world, Jacqueline Bouvier Kennedy was called a porcelain princess, an American beauty, and Queen of America. To the American people, however, she was simply Jackie. Her aristocratic manner and movie star appeal captivated young women, who imitated her every move, and she attracted adoring fans everywhere she went. Being married to John F. Kennedy, the United States' popular president, only heightened her fame. Jackie had tremendous creative talents, including writing, painting, and photography, but it was her beauty that charmed most people.

Jackie Kennedy became America's aristocracy and gave the nation a taste of royalty. When she visited with Queen Elizabeth in London, British newspapers were quoted as saying, "For the first time America has in Jacqueline Kennedy what they have always lacked—majesty."[31]

Yet beneath that shining exterior, there was a young woman who tended to be introverted and solitary. Jackie never sought acclaim nor did she enjoy the spotlight or public scrutiny. In fact, she fought the media's intense probing into her personal life until her death on May 19, 1994.

Youth

Jacqueline Bouvier was born on July 28, 1929, in Southhampton, New York. Her father was New York stockbroker John V. Bouvier III and her mother was Janet Lee Bouvier. The couple separated when Jackie was eight and divorced when she was thirteen. Later her mother married Hugh D. Auchincloss, another stockbroker.

Jackie was deeply affected by her parents' separation. She adored her handsome father, known as "Black Jack." He was fun, generous, and warm. On the other hand, her mother was careful

Understanding the importance of training her horse helped young Jackie (left) realize the importance of her own education.

with her money and cool to her oldest daughter. During the years after the divorce, Jackie's Bouvier relatives watched helplessly as the girl began to withdraw, becoming moody and aloof.

During her elementary school years, Jackie attended the Chapin School, an exclusive private school in New York City. Friends from those days called her obstinate and independent. They said her attention often seemed to wander and that she didn't like having others tell her what to do. Many of her teachers had a real problem with Jackie. The girl was difficult to discipline and spent a great deal of time in the headmistress's office.

The school's headmistress, Ethel Stringfellow, was more tolerant of Jackie's wandering mind. Stringfellow knew that horses were very important to Jackie. And the headmistress finally got through to her by talking about horses, that even thoroughbreds needed training just as Jackie needed an education. The headmistress once admitted, "I mightn't have kept Jacqueline except that she had the most inquiring mind we'd had in the school in thirty-five years."[32]

In 1951, Jackie graduated from George Washington University in Washington, D.C., where she proved herself an artistically gifted and brilliant student, proficient in French and speaking Spanish and Italian well. Once out of school, she made a career for herself as a journalist, working for the *Washington Times-Herald*. There she was responsible for a daily column that included photographs of ordinary people and their answers to questions like "What do you think of marriage?" "What's your idea of the perfect mate?" When she tired of questioning people on the street or in supermarkets, she turned to public figures like congressmen. Her combination of intelligence and beauty attracted a handsome, up-and-coming senator from Massachusetts named John F. Kennedy.

Courtship and Marriage

Later, John Kennedy confessed that when he met Jackie at a dinner party in 1951, he knew he wanted to marry her. They started dating, but Jackie called it a spasmodic courtship, because JFK was often in Massachusetts campaigning. She devised ways to attract him, even translating and summarizing a book about Indochina from French to English for him. She also bought him books and used her newspaper column to catch his attention with questions about marriage.

John Kennedy was thirty-five when he met Jackie. He had already decided that he wanted to be president and tried to maintain a public image of what the American public wanted in a leader. He knew that voters preferred their presidents to be married, and although JFK's name had been connected often with other women, none was as suitable a mate as Jackie. She was beautiful, well educated, and from a fine family—the perfect wife for a candidate.

On September 12, 1953, Jackie married John Kennedy in Newport, Rhode Island. The couple made their home in Georgetown. Jackie's new life as a politician's wife was a revelation to her. She had no idea what marriage to JFK would entail, but she desperately wanted her life to be centered in the home and family. Jackie explained to reporters, "My life revolves around my husband. His life is my life. It is up to me to make his home a haven, a refuge . . . but never let the arrangements ruffle him, never let him see that it is work. . . . I want to take such good care of my husband that whatever he is doing, he can do it better because he has me."[33]

Part of helping her husband involved playing a role in his political bids as well. Although she was perfectly happy to work behind the scenes, Jackie did not like the rough-and-tumble world of political rallies. What she liked even less was the publicity that went along with the politics. She once told one of her Auchincloss relatives, "Nothing disturbs me as much as interviewers and journalists. That's the trouble with the public eye. But if you make your living in public office, you're the property of every tax-paying citizen. Your life is an open book."[34]

Jackie was a perfect political wife: beautiful, well educated, and from a fine family.

Witty, warm, and interesting with her own group of acquaintances, Jackie became cold and withdrawn when forced into situations where there were crowds or groups of people she did not know. She preferred small sociable gatherings at home rather than huge parties or receptions, and she enjoyed talking about her daughter, Caroline, born in 1957, rather than politics. Eventually, though, Jackie learned that being a good wife for John Kennedy meant she would have to campaign with him.

Campaigning for the Presidency

The idea of campaigning was so repugnant to Jackie that at first she refused to do it. She hated the idea of shaking hands and talking to total strangers, but she knew that if she rebelled against her husband's all-consuming love of politics, she risked her marriage. After months of planning, Jackie finally got excited at the thought of her husband being president. During the 1960 campaign, she traveled extensively with him, even though she was pregnant with her second child. Her role was simple. She said, "I show up and smile . . . and sometimes I might say a few words, but that's all Jack [JFK was also known as Jack] says I have to do."[35] Most of the time those few words were in French or Spanish or even a little Polish, depending on the audience. After Jackie spoke to the people in their language in one Italian community, the older ladies gathered around her, hugging her as if she were family.

Jackie appeared in each primary state with her husband. His toughest opposition was in Wisconsin and West Virginia, and JFK's mother and sister held tea parties and barbecues there to draw people. Jackie, however, had other ideas. In West Virginia, she traveled to miners' shacks where she visited with their wives and told them about her husband's campaign. In Neillsville, Wisconsin, she spoke on a radio program and made a short statement about JFK. She said, "He has served his country fourteen years in the Navy and Congress. He cares deeply about the welfare of this nation, and as President, he will make the greatest contribution to its future."[36]

Jackie's way of campaigning touched people. Her reserved and mysterious personality appealed to the crowds, and they responded when she visited their homes and spoke their language. Charles Peters, editor of the *Washington Monthly*, said, "What amazed me most, I think, was the way people reacted to Jackie. I first got the sense of Jackie's emerging popularity, of what was happening in American society. There was no question . . . they identified with the Princess. You could just tell they wanted

Jackie played a major role in her husband's presidential campaign, traveling to each primary state with him.

Jackie . . . they were looking for an aristocratic image."[37] When JFK was elected president in 1960, he admitted that his wife had played a major role.

Living a Public Life

Although she had been committed to working for her husband's election, Jackie hated the loss of her privacy after moving into the White House. As a result, she became even more reserved in an effort to prevent invasion of her personal life. She worried especially about protecting her daughter, Caroline, and her son, John F. Kennedy Jr., born in 1960. In the hopes of maintaining their privacy, she required

An intensely private person, Jackie was especially protective of her children, John Jr. (left) and Caroline.

that all members of the White House staff sign an agreement never to speak to the press or talk about their jobs working with the Kennedys. To one staff member, she wrote, "I feel strongly that publicity in this era has gotten completely out of hand—and you must really protect the privacy of me and my children."[38]

Restoration Project

Once she had secured her children's privacy (as best she could), Jackie went to work on her first White House project. Familiar with many of the impressive homes around the nation, Jackie was appalled at the state of the presidential mansion, saying it looked like it had been furnished by discount stores. She decided to take it upon herself to restore the White House. She said,

> "Presidents' wives have an obligation to contribute something. People who visit the White House see practically noth-

ing that dates before 1900 . . . people should see things that develop their sense of history. . . . Everything in the White House must have a reason for being there. . . . It would be a sacrilege merely to redecorate. . . . It must be restored."[39]

She formed a Fine Arts Committee and asked Henry Du Pont, a well-known expert on American antiques, to be the chairman. Jackie wanted only the best antiques representing early America. Together, she and DuPont made lists of people who might have any suitable furniture and would be willing to donate it to the renovation work. Jackie learned of a doctor in New York who had a mirror that once belonged to George Washington and a newspaper publisher who owned a portrait of Benjamin Franklin. She personally spoke with both men, among many others, and was able to add their treasures to the White House's collection.

Estimating that the restoration would cost more than $2 million, Jackie formed the White House Historical Association to raise the necessary funds. She also decided to publish a White House guidebook to sell to tourists, the proceeds of which would help finance her project. Eventually, that small book paid for the restoration many times over.

First Lady Jacqueline Kennedy (center) sits with officials of the American Institute of Interior Design in the White House ground floor library. The Institute sponsored the library's refurbishment.

Jackie unveiled her project on February 14, 1962, when CBS aired a tour of the entire mansion. More than 46 million Americans watched as Jackie walked through the newly redecorated rooms. Without a script, she related the history of each room and pointed out the new furnishings. The restoration project and tour turned out to be a major public relations victory for both Jackie and the United States.

Around the World

In the summer of 1961, Jackie accompanied her husband on a state visit to France, and almost overnight she became an international sensation. Parisians went wild at the sight of her. They shouted her name and called "Vive Jackie!" wherever she went. Although people liked Jackie in the United States, JFK's sister Jean Smith said, "I think the fact that she went to Europe and created a stir . . . was a surprise. Up to that point she was just his [John Kennedy's] wife. . . . Afterwards, she realized she had great influence on people."[40]

It was during this same trip that the Kennedys met in Vienna, Austria, with Nikita and Nina Khrushchev. It was the first meeting between the U.S. president and the leader of the Soviet Union. Khrushchev verbally lashed out at John Kennedy during their meetings, making the president appear to be the weaker of the two leaders.

The crowds that gathered outside the Schonbrun Palace, where the meeting took place, were more interested in Jackie than they were in the heads of state. They began to chant Jackie's name. Jackie got up and walked to the window and waved at the people below. The Khrushchevs were not happy that the people wanted to see only the American first lady; no one was calling for Nina. In a truly diplomatic move, however, Jackie turned and called Nina to the window. Immediately the crowd outside began to shout "Jackie, Nina." The small crisis was over.

Goodwill Mission

After Jackie proved her diplomatic skills in Vienna, the president realized she was a political asset and asked her to make a goodwill visit to India and Pakistan in March 1962. On Jackie's first evening in New Delhi, Indira Gandhi taught her the traditional Indian greeting, palms together as if in prayer. When she greeted the Indian public this way, the crowds chanted "Hail Jackie!" and called her the Queen of America.

While she was in India, Jackie attempted to follow the customs of the local people. She wore the traditional Indian tilak, a dot of

Mrs. Jacqueline Kennedy (left) and Mrs. Nina Khrushchev smile and wave from a window of the Schonbrun Palace in Vienna, Austria, in 1961.

red paint on her forehead, and donned cloth slippers when she visited temples. She took a boat trip down the country's sacred Ganges River, rode an elephant, and visited the Taj Mahal. Her respect for their customs won her the undying admiration of the people there.

President Kennedy called the trip to India semi-official and said Jackie was acting as his representative because she had visited the nation's leaders, including Prime Minister Nehru and district governors. Although there were a few critics who called the trip a waste of taxpayers' money, the president was impressed with Jackie's performance. He said, "Jackie took all the bitterness out of our relations with India. . . . Jackie did a good job."[41]

Traveling abroad to represent the United States had given Jackie prestige. Her desire to be more important to her husband in his administration grew, and it wouldn't be long before Jackie proved her skills and influence under extreme conditions.

The Cuban Missile Crisis

In October 1962, the United States faced the threat of a nuclear war. The Central Intelligence Agency (CIA) informed President Kennedy that the Soviet Union had installed nuclear missiles on the island of Cuba, a country ninety miles off the coast of Florida, and pointed them at the United States. President Kennedy ordered an air and sea quarantine on shipping American goods into Cuba and warned the Soviet Union that he would take drastic action if the missiles were not removed. In an address to the nation, the president said, "It shall be the policy of this nation to regard any missile launched from Cuba . . . as an attack by the Soviet Union on the United States requiring a full retaliatory response."[42]

During the terrifying period called the Cuban Missile Crisis, the president suggested that Jackie leave Washington, D.C., and go to a place where she would be safer. Jackie refused, preferring to stay close to her husband. She knew her presence comforted him, but she also played a greater role, that of adviser.

Some of the president's cabinet members remembered her presence and remarked about her influence on her husband. Robert S. McNamara, former secretary of defense, said, "Jackie is one of the most underrated women in the country. She is extraordinarily astute politically. . . . The President consulted her on any number of issues. . . . JFK turned to his wife for advice whenever a crisis arose. . . . He would talk to her about it and she would talk to him . . . she would advise him."[43] Five days after the crisis began, the Soviet Union promised to remove the missiles from Cuba.

Jackie advised her husband about other things as well. For example, she strongly supported normalizing trade relations with the Soviet Union, particularly regarding the sale of produce to the starving Soviet people. Jackie also played a role in President Kennedy's supporting a Soviet treaty to stop testing nuclear weapons. Jackie wholeheartedly pushed her husband to agree to the terms, and he listened to her even when others disagreed. Of her influence, one Kennedy associate said, "First Ladies know presidents better, and often influence them more, than most people think."[44]

Tragedy Brings Them Closer

In August 1963, Jackie, pregnant with her third child, went to visit the Kennedy family at Hyannis Port, Massachusetts. During the visit, she was rushed to Otis Air Force Base Hospital, where she gave birth to a little boy whom she and President Kennedy named Patrick Bouvier Kennedy. The baby, though, had been born six weeks early and suffered from a problem with his lungs common to many premature infants. Doctors placed Patrick in an intensive care unit, but he died a few hours later.

In their sorrow, Jackie and her husband drew close. The couple, who had rarely displayed warmth in their relationship, were now seen holding hands. A month after Patrick's death, Jackie ran to meet the president's helicopter when it landed at the White House. Close family friend Ben Bradlee said it "was the most affectionate embrace we had ever seen them give each other. They [were] not normally demonstrative."[45]

President and Mrs. Kennedy leave Otis Air Force Base Hospital after the death of their third child, Patrick Bouvier Kennedy.

Last Campaign

Their newfound closeness continued when JFK began to make plans for the 1964 presidential election. He knew that Jackie's impact on the people could help him, and when he asked her to campaign with him, she readily agreed. One of their first stops was Dallas, Texas, in November, mainly because the president was not very popular there. Even with a Texan as vice president, he had barely carried the state in 1960.

On November 22, 1963, the couple flew to Dallas's Love Field. Because the weather was warm and sunny, President Kennedy ordered the bubble top removed from his car. The couple rode in a navy-blue convertible accompanied by Governor John Connally and his wife. At 1:30 the motorcade arrived at downtown Dallas's Dealey Plaza. As it passed a building called the Texas School Book Depository, Lady Bird Johnson, wife of the vice president, who was riding two cars behind the president and first lady, said she heard a loud crack, followed by two more. It was fireworks, she thought.

At the same time, Jackie turned to look at her husband when she heard a noise she thought was a car backfiring. "And I just turned and looked at him. . . . I remember thinking he looked as if he had a slight headache . . . then, he . . . put his hand to his forehead and fell into my lap." Realizing that her husband had been shot, Jackie screamed, "My God, they've killed Jack! They've killed my husband!"[46]

The president died moments later. In the hours and days that followed, the true courage and dignity of Jacqueline Kennedy became apparent to everyone. When Lyndon Johnson was sworn in as president, Jackie stood beside him, still wearing her blood-stained suit. No longer shunning publicity, she let the world watch her mourn her husband.

President Kennedy's death was a shock and a tragedy for his family and for the nation. They knew he was coming to Texas in an attempt to make friends and solicit their endorsement. Mary Barelli Gallagher, Jackie's personal secretary, recalled walking into Jackie's private compartment on the president's airplane, Air Force One, during the trip back to Washington. Gallagher wrote, "There on the bed lay one of Jackie's gloves. No longer spotlessly white and soft as it was that morning; but now completely blackened by her husband's blood, dried stiff . . . it rested on a newspaper, which carried the large bold headline: 'Dallas welcomes JFK.'"[47]

Three days after the assassination, world leaders gathered in Washington, D.C., for the funeral of John F. Kennedy. Even though the Secret Service objected, Jackie joined them and her

Jackie displayed great courage and dignity following her husband's assassination, earning the respect and admiration of many around the world.

husband's brothers in walking behind her husband's coffin the eight blocks to the church for the funeral.

Jackie had planned every detail of the funeral. And in doing so, she allowed everyone to join her in saying good-bye to her husband. Before the president's death, many people had seen her only as a beautiful face, the wife of a popular man. However, in the days that followed, her own courage and nobility gained her the respect of many. Larry O'Brien, one of President Kennedy's political advisers, said,

> All in all, I don't think I have ever experienced the kind of courage she demonstrated, first at the hospital in Dallas, and on that plane to Washington, and then during the funeral. . . . On the whole she acquitted herself magnificently and became a symbol for all of us, of great nobility in an age of general impoverishment of the soul.[48]

After the White House

After her husband's assassination, Jackie desperately wanted a quiet, private place to live and raise her children. That wish would never come true, however; she was much too well known for that. Unable to fade from public view, Jackie again hit the campaign trail in 1968, this time for her brother-in-law, Robert Kennedy. She worried about his safety, however, and once said at a New York dinner party, "Do you know what I think will happen to Bobby? The same thing that happened to Jack. There is too much hatred in this country, and more people hate Bobby than hated Jack."[49]

Ultimately, her words came true. Robert Kennedy was assassinated on June 5, 1968 (he died on June 6). It was an event that terrified and infuriated Jackie. She told a friend, "I hate this country. I despise America and I don't want my children to live here anymore. If they are killing Kennedys, my children are . . . targets. . . . I want to get out of this country."[50]

In 1969 she shocked many people in the United States by marrying Aristotle Onassis, a wealthy Greek shipowner in his sixties. On his private island of Skorpios, Jackie and her children found some of the seclusion she had been seeking.

Picture here in March 1977, Jacqueline Bouvier Kennedy Onassis died in May 1994 at the age of sixty-four.

After only a few years of marriage, though, Jackie separated from Onassis, and he died in 1975. Following the separation, she moved to New York City and went to work for Viking Press and then Doubleday as an editor. Even as she shied from reporters and all kinds of publicity, Jackie was the subject of countless articles and books. The public never tired of hearing about what she was doing. Her death at age sixty-four on May 19, 1994, of non-Hodgkin's lymphoma came as a shock to the nation, for she was still America's royalty.

CHAPTER 4

Betty Bloomer Ford: Outspoken Women's Advocate

When naming Betty Bloomer Ford Woman of the Year in 1975, *Newsweek* magazine cited her plainspokenness. Mrs. Ford's policy on answering questions was simple: "When somebody asks you how you stand on an issue, you're very foolish if you try to beat around the bush—you just meet yourself going around the bush the other way."[51]

She let the president, her husband Gerald Ford, know her opinions and worked hard to influence his decisions, especially those concerning equal rights for women. Political researcher Louis Harris credited Betty's candid manner for her husband's support among the young and independent voters. And many people believed that Betty's honesty helped rebuild the trust in leadership the nation lost after President Richard Nixon's resignation in 1974.

Betty's independence and support for equal rights also offered hope to women who had long been waiting for a spokesperson as vocal and influential as she. Being in the White House gave Betty a forum, and she was ready and willing to use it. After her years as first lady, she courageously made public her admission into the Long Beach Naval Hospital's Alcohol and Drug Rehabilitation Service. Open as always, she didn't hide her addiction, and her popularity soared.

Betty Grows Up

Elizabeth "Betty" Ann Bloomer was born on April 8, 1918, in Chicago. The family moved to Grand Rapids, Michigan, when she was two. There her father worked as a traveling salesman. Betty's mother drove her to perfection in everything she did. Betty flourished under her mother's encouragement, found it a challenge, and learned to do her best. Even as a child, Betty's personality sparkled, and her mother channeled that exuberance into dance classes, which became the love of Betty's life. She began taking lessons at age eight and by fourteen was teaching youngsters herself.

For two summers, when she was eighteen and nineteen, Betty studied at the Bennington School of Dance in Vermont. There she worked with Martha Graham, a famous choreographer. Because she admired Graham's style of dance, Betty decided to study under her in New York. At age twenty, Betty moved to New York City, where she attended Graham's school and lived in a small apartment in New York, working days as a model and dancing at night. She eventually danced at Carnegie Hall, but she lacked total dedication and never advanced to the top group of Graham's dancers.

Disappointed, she returned to Grand Rapids, where she taught dance. In 1942, she married Bill Warren, whom she had known since childhood. She soon discovered, though, that he could not hold a job and preferred the company of his friends in the bar to his wife. By 1947, they were divorced.

Future First Lady Betty Ford (left) loved dancing from an early age.

Betty's naturally effervescent personality kept her from being despondent. She took a long look at her life and decided what her goals would be for the future. Betty said, "I knew I had to make a life for myself and figured I'd probably do that in the fashion field. . . . I was so fed up with marriage that I knew I'd never consider another one."[52] That resolution changed when she met the former football star and lawyer Gerald Ford.

Early Life with Jerry

Jerry Ford had been a local high school football hero and was well known in Grand Rapids. He and Betty had run into each other often at the country club. After her divorce, the two began to date, and in a short time, Gerald Ford and Betty were engaged to be married. Jerry was campaigning for a seat in the House of Representatives. While he visited people all over the district, Betty spent her time putting up posters and recruiting more volunteers to lick stamps and stuff envelopes. They took just enough of a break to be married on October 15, 1948; she was thirty and he was thirty-five. The next day they went to Owosso, Michigan, because Jerry wanted to hear presidential candidate Tom Dewey speak. And by the next week, they were in Ann Arbor because Jerry had a political meeting. Traipsing all over the state instead of going on a honeymoon gave Betty a taste of what being a politician's wife was all about.

On November 2, 1948, Jerry was elected to the House of Representatives as a Republican, and the Fords moved to Washington, D.C. They found a one-bedroom apartment on Q Street in Georgetown and Betty settled in.

As Jerry's seniority in the House grew, so did his responsibilities, meaning more time away from home. By 1957, the Ford family had grown to include three boys and a girl, and Betty discovered that being married to a politician meant raising a family without her husband much of the time. She enjoyed her children but found herself discontented. Her husband said later, "It put a strain on the marriage. . . . I was all over the country and sometimes overseas and with four active children, Betty had a tough obligation. . . . She had to be not only the mother but the father."[53]

The Pain Begins

The stress of caring for her family finally took its toll. One night in 1964, Betty reached across her kitchen cabinet and felt a searing pain down her neck to her left arm. Throughout the night she suffered, and by morning the arm had gone numb. Jerry rushed her

Betty quickly learned what being a politician's wife was all about; there wasn't even time for a honeymoon when she married Gerald Ford in 1948.

to the hospital, where doctors told her she had a pinched nerve. They put her in traction, using a series of weights designed to stretch her muscles, for two weeks. When she was released from the hospital, she couldn't stand up straight and had to hold her left arm across her chest. The pain in her neck and back was constant, so doctors prescribed pain medication. Betty began to rely on prescription medicine to get her through each day.

Six years later, as a result of the continual pain, the stress of caring for her family, and the anger at being alone so often, Betty suffered a nervous collapse and started seeing a psychiatrist twice a week. He taught her to take time for herself and find an outlet for her emotions. Analysis helped her gain confidence and look honestly at her problems. "Now it all seems obvious," she said later. "I was resentful of Jerry's being gone so much. I was feeling terribly neglected."[54] And of course, there was the neck pain, which worsened when she later developed arthritis. To overcome these problems and at her doctor's suggestion, she added daily doses of tranquilizers to the pain pills.

Appointments

In 1973 Vice President Spiro Agnew resigned from his position after being accused of taking bribes. President Nixon, who was also under suspicion of misusing his power, needed a vice president who was above reproach. People started whispering that Jerry Ford was the perfect man for the job. Betty, however, thought differently. Jerry had been minority leader in the House since 1965, a powerful position as the head of all House Republicans. Knowing that her husband's role in the House was important to the Nixon administration, Betty told her daughter, "Your father is much too valuable in the House. . . . The President would never take him out."[55] However, she was wrong.

The announcement came on October 12, 1973. As soon as she found out, Betty hurried to the East Room of the White House, but there was no place for her to sit. First Lady Pat Nixon slid over and the two women shared a chair as they listened to President Nixon appoint Jerry Ford vice president.

Wife of the President

A short ten months later, President Nixon also resigned, when the country learned that he had known about and endorsed the break-in at Democratic National Party headquarters in Washington, D.C.'s Watergate Hotel. As a result, on August 9, 1974, Gerald Ford became president of the United States.

Although Betty was absolutely certain that her husband would make a fine president, she was worried about what kind of first lady she would be. She admitted feeling terrified. *Time* magazine quotes her as saying, "I really didn't want to come here [the White House]. I was afraid because of the social demands, and I didn't think of it as a meaningful position for me."[56]

The first few days were especially frightening. On her second day as first lady, Betty learned that Jordan's King Hussein and his wife Queen Alia would visit the White House in six days. Everything had to be arranged, from floral decorations to seating to menus. Betty threw herself into the project, and the visit went perfectly. The results amazed her. Betty said later, "You never know what you can do until you have to do it."[57]

Reporters soon began asking the new first lady what her project would be. She told them she was interested in the arts, women's rights, working with handicapped children, and encouraging better treatment for the elderly. One thing she didn't want was to be a duplicate of those who had served before her. She was determined to choose a cause that would uniquely reflect her own views. "I wanted to be a good First Lady," she said, ". . . but I didn't believe I had to do every single thing some previous [Presidents'] wives had done. . . . I'm just going to be Betty Bloomer Ford . . . might as well have a good time doing it."[58]

ERA and Women's Rights

Betty's outspoken views soon caught the attention of news broadcasters who claimed that becoming first lady had changed her into a woman who said exactly what she believed. Betty denied that,

With Betty at his side, Gerald Ford is sworn in as president of the United States in August 1974.

First Lady Betty Ford dances with King Hussein of Jordan. King Hussein and his wife were the first guests of the Ford White House in August 1974.

however, saying it "wasn't so much that the White House altered me in any essential way, as that I found the resources with which to respond to . . . challenges."[59] One of those challenges was the issue of women's rights.

As wife of the vice president, Betty had already been involved with passage of the proposed Equal Rights Amendment (ERA) to the Constitution. The ERA stipulated that women would receive equal pay if they did the same work as men, would have the same access to jobs and education, and would gain the right to play sports and join the military. When she realized that her new position as first lady might carry some influence, Betty didn't back down from calling important political figures across the nation and getting them involved.

She worked hardest to convince her husband, President Ford, to support women's rights. In January 1975, he signed an order establishing a National Commission on the Observance of International Women's Year. This move established presidential support for women and the ERA. Betty felt this step moved the United States toward correcting the inequality between the sexes. (The amendment, however, was defeated in 1982.)

First Lady Betty Ford was an outspoken advocate for equal rights.

Not everyone believed that the ERA was a good thing. A group of conservative women led by Phyllis Schlafly considered Betty's efforts for equal rights misguided. They organized the Eagle Forum and traveled across the country arguing that the amendment would change laws on marriage, force young women into military combat, and bring about laws compelling men and women to share the same public bathrooms. They accused Betty of making the mothers and housewives across the nation feel that their lives were worthless. Betty responded by saying,

> In fact, being a good housewife seems to me a much tougher job than going to the office and getting paid for it. What man could afford to pay for all the things a wife does, when she's a cook, a mistress, a chauffeur, a nurse, a baby-sitter? But because of this, I believe women ought to have equal rights, equal social security, equal opportunity for education and an equal chance to establish credit.[60]

Her work for women's rights extended beyond the ERA as well. To her delight, Betty found she was even capable of influencing her husband in his appointments to public office. It was because of Betty's views that President Ford chose Carla Hill as housing and urban development secretary and appointed Anne Armstrong ambassador to Britain. Betty once explained her method of lobbying the President: "Evenings we usually spend together, both working while we sit in the den. . . . You might call it 'pillow talk.'. . . I definitely think I have influenced him on women's issues. There's a woman in the Cabinet—and I suggested that. Now if I can get a woman on the Supreme Court, I'll be batting a thousand."[61]

An Outspoken First Lady

At times, however, Betty's outspoken views caused problems. In one particular instance, her forthright manner caused controversy when she was interviewed on the television program *60 Minutes* in August 1975. She gave completely candid answers to Morley Safer's questions about drugs, abortion, divorce, and premarital sex. She admitted that she might have tried marijuana if she were of the '70s generation and also suggested that, although she did not advocate premarital sex, it might lower the divorce rate. When Safer asked what she would do if she discovered that her daughter was having an affair, she answered, "Well, frankly, I wouldn't be surprised. I think she's a perfectly normal human being, like all girls."[62]

Following the interview, the mail poured in. Religious leaders wrote that they were outraged, and newspaper editorials screamed that Betty condoned immorality. After a few days, however, the tone of the letters received at the White House changed. Those who agreed with Betty's views began to write too, and soon 75 percent of the mail was in support of the first lady. Political researcher Louis Harris said,

> Mrs. Ford's outspoken statements have won support from those younger and more independent elements in the electorate who are indispensable to her husband in a contest for the White House next fall. Betty Ford has a wide and deep following . . . and must be judged a solid asset.[63]

Battling Breast Cancer

Betty's popularity also soared when she opened her private life to public scrutiny and shared her experience with breast surgery. On September 26, 1974, during a routine exam, doctors discovered a lump in Betty's breast. Two days later her right breast was removed, along with some muscle tissue and several lymph nodes.

Betty soon began receiving cards and letters from women across the nation who had responded to her example and gone for an exam. As a result, some of their lives had been saved by early detection of cancer.

Betty tried to look at her surgery as just another milestone in her life. She told herself she was still a whole person, that life is so much more important than the loss of a breast, and that it could have been much worse. Her positive attitude was further encouraged by the stories of women her experience had helped. In June 1975, Betty told her secretary how she had felt when she was told she had breast cancer:

> It knocked the wind out of me. . . . I guess the cancer operation was a terrible jolt, but it was also the first sign I had of how powerful this position [of first lady] is. My ex-

Betty Ford celebrated her twenty-sixth wedding anniversary with her husband not long after undergoing breast cancer surgery.

perience sent the message out. I've had letters from people who found they had cancer. . . . If you can save one life, you're glad. If you can save many, you're really happy.[64]

A Growing Addiction

Cancer wasn't Betty's only health problem during her years in the White House. In fact, her growing dependence on pain medication was becoming more and more obvious. In *Newsweek*, one acquaintance was quoted as saying that she had seen Betty appear drugged. And once, her secretary asked that Betty hold off on taking a pill she was about to swallow until after her speech, telling her she didn't come off as natural when she had taken the medication. Still, Betty refused to recognize her dependence. After all, she rationalized, physicians with the highest credentials were prescribing the medicine for her.

Despite her growing addiction, she remained active and didn't let her pain, or the drugs, stop her from giving everything she had to her husband's 1976 campaign. She traveled across the country to ceremonies, dedications, or any other place people gathered. She spoke time after time, greeted total strangers, and spent days away from home. Of that campaign, she wrote later, "I hadn't wanted Jerry to be President, but I had long since accepted his decision to run. . . . I felt he would be the best man for the job and I was willing to take on four more years in the White House."[65]

Presidential Campaign

Since Gerald Ford was very busy as president, Betty considered it her job to do much of the campaigning. She tried to see as many people as possible and tell them about her husband's integrity, leadership, and honesty. She went to Indiana to the opening of a children's museum, to Florida to a school dedication ceremony, and to Texas, where she spoke to truckers on a citizens band radio.

Throughout the weeks and months of travel, Betty's popularity held. There were many campaign buttons that said "I Love Betty" or "Elect Betty's Husband" or "Keep Betty in the White House." "I loved it," she said; "I'd be dishonest if I said it didn't please me. I hadn't expected it, but so long as it was forthcoming, I enjoyed it."[66]

At each stop, Betty had to give a speech. At first, she was frightened, but as she gave more speeches she gained confidence, ultimately speaking without notes and addressing many controversial issues. Of the value of her campaigning, she said, "Proceeding on the assumption that people like to see a candidate's family, a candidate's wife shakes hands, holds babies, visits with old folks,

Betty's popularity remained strong as she traveled throughout the country campaigning for her husband in 1976.

drinks gallons of coffee, gives a little speech or does a little dance, and hopes she's more of a plus than a minus to her husband."[67]

Even though Betty enjoyed some aspects of campaigning, there were other parts she didn't like. Mostly she disliked that critics and comedians portrayed Jerry as unintelligent. But Betty carried on, strongly raising her voice in defense of her husband.

Addictions Begin to Show

At times, however, Betty's voice seemed anything but strong. At a reception in June, her voice slurred and she referred to herself as "president." People began to wonder if Betty was exhausted from so many speeches and receptions. Two days after the June reception, Betty visited her former high school in Grand Rapids, where she spoke very slowly and was noticeably confused. She spoke of Ronald Reagan, who was just another candidate at the time, as "President Reagan." Something was obviously wrong.

Press Secretary Sheila Weidenfeld, concerned over symptoms she had observed, turned to Betty's doctor, who believed that the first lady's slurred speech and confusion were from the pain she suffered. Her neck pain had been made worse by arthritis and the days of hard campaigning. Despite the pain and the addiction, however, Betty continued to be her cheerful self. Writing about those days in her book, Sheila Weidenfeld said,

> [Betty] seemed all right. She looked all right too. I can't get over how she does it. She has, I guess, managed a perfect way of pulling it off, masquerading as "fine"—indeed sometimes even radiant, sparkly—while actually enduring great pain. . . . Yet no one would have been able to tell. . . . She says that the masquerade helps her feel better, forget the discomfort a little.[68]

The discomfort and stress brought on by life in the White House ended when Gerald Ford lost the 1976 election to Jimmy Carter. Although Betty was disappointed, she was also relieved. As she looked back over that day, she wrote in her memoirs, "My conviction that my husband was the better man, my dissatisfaction that we hadn't been able to win, these were real. But so was my vision of a soon to be restored private life, and my relief that our ordeal was over."[69]

Life Goes On

Immediately after Jimmy Carter's inauguration, Betty and Jerry Ford began building a new house and a new life together. They chose to live in Palm Springs, California, because the dry climate was good for Betty's arthritis. Believing that when he retired she would have more of Jerry's time, Betty seemed happy at first. But her husband soon accepted a job lecturing on college campuses nationwide, often leaving Betty home alone. The depression that followed made her turn more and more to alcohol. This time, though, her symptoms were obvious.

Betty's daughter Susan watched as her mother developed a serious addiction. Summoning help from a physician, Susan convinced her father to try to persuade Betty to get help. With the doctor and several others, Jerry talked to Betty and helped her realize that the medication was interfering with her life. Each family member related an incident when her drug use had embarrassed them. One son told her he was afraid to have children who might see their grandmother drugged. This approach, called intervention, galvanized Betty into action.

A week later, she checked in to the Long Beach Naval Hospital's Alcohol and Drug Rehabilitation Service. There, she finally realized just how dependent on drugs and alcohol she had become. Betty began the battle of her life. She wrote, "When you're suffering from alcoholism, or any other drug dependency, your self-esteem gets so low you're sure nobody would want to bother with you. I think intervention works because suddenly you realize that somebody is willing to bother, somebody cares."[70]

When she first arrived at the center, Betty expected special treatment because she was a former first lady. That never happened, though, and Betty learned a valuable lesson—everyone is equal in rehab. When she gained sobriety and was clean of drugs, it was just as much of an accomplishment as it would have been for anyone else.

The Betty Ford Center

Betty's own experience and her desire to help others led her to build the Betty Ford Center for Drug and Alcohol Rehabilitation in 1982.

Following her successful treatment, Betty wanted to share what she had learned with others. With the help of her many friends and family, she built a rehabilitation center of her own that would offer the same kind of treatment she had received. Called the Betty Ford Center for Drug and Alcohol Rehabilitation, it opened in 1982 in Rancho Mirage, California.

Betty took an active role in the project. She often visited patients, especially celebrities or others who might expect preferential treatment. She assured everyone who came to the center that they would achieve sobriety because they had earned it, not because someone had handed it to them.

Although Betty knew she was helping people, she didn't feel it was because she was special. She said,

> Sometimes I'm asked if I feel I have a mission. I don't. I'm not that presumptuous. . . . But I do think people relate to someone who has the same problems they have, and who overcomes them. And I think God has allowed me—along with thousands of others—to carry a message, a message that says, there's help out there, and you, too, can be a survivor. . . . Look at me.[71]

As in all her other affairs, Betty Bloomer Ford spoke out, not only for herself but because she wanted to help other people. As a mother, a wife, and a first lady, she had opened her life and given of herself to those less fortunate. Betty Ford's creed was simple: "Trust and believe in yourself. . . . What is important in our lives is not so much what we have in the way of intelligence or talent, but what we do with these gifts."[72]

Chapter 5

Barbara Pierce Bush: America's First Mother

Commentators often said that Barbara Bush looked more like her husband's mother than his wife, but it was that down-to-earth, motherly quality that appealed to the nation. Americans connected with Barbara, associating her with their mothers or their grandmothers. Through more than fifty years of marriage, the death of her second child, several national campaigns, and more than thirty moves, Barbara Bush maintained her position that her family comes first.

After President Bush's first hundred days in office, traditionally a period of close observation, polls showed that Barbara Bush's rating among the people was higher than either her husband's or Vice President Dan Quayle's. There was no doubt about it, America loved Barbara Bush. She received an average of three thousand letters a week and once quipped, "I'll tell you, my mail tells me a lot of fat, white-haired, wrinkled ladies are tickled pink."[73]

American women looked at Barbara and saw themselves, their mothers, their grandmothers, and Barbara wasn't afraid to use that quality to reach people. Nationwide, people sensed her genuineness and honesty. And they loved her for it. She totally charmed the American people, who opened their hearts and took her in as more than a first lady. Barbara Bush became first mother to the country.

Her Youth

Barbara Pierce was born the third of four children on June 8, 1925. She grew up in Rye, New York, a community of around eight thousand, just outside New York City. The town consisted of a few stores and a movie theater, where most of the children spent their Saturdays. Rye was a place where neighbors knew one another and children played jump rope, rode bicycles, and teased each other like children everywhere.

Marvin Pierce, Barbara's father, was the center of her life. He was a man with a wonderful sense of humor, which he passed on

In First Lady Barbara Bush, American women saw themselves, their mothers, and their grandmothers.

to his daughter. Barbara's mother, Pauline, on the other hand, never enjoyed her life and was always waiting for something better to happen. It was Pauline's attitude from which Barbara says she learned a valuable lesson: Enjoy each day as it comes. She said, "You have two choices in life: You can like what you do or you can dislike it. I have chosen to like it."[74]

At fifteen, Barbara went away to school. She spent the school year at Ashley Hall in Charleston, South Carolina, where she was an excellent student. During the summers and on school holidays, she came home. It was on one of those trips home, Christmas of her junior year, that she met George Bush. Barbara said,

It was Christmas when I was sixteen—1941—and I was having a wonderful time. I was at a vacation dance in Greenwich, Connecticut, seeing friends I hadn't seen since summer and wearing a pretty, bright new red-and-green dress. Jack Wozencraft, a boy I had grown up with, cut in on my dancing partner and took me to meet a wonderful-looking young boy who he said wanted to meet me, a boy named Poppy [George] Bush.[75]

It was the beginning of a relationship of mutual respect and deep affection. They were still very young, though, so George joined the navy and Barbara went back to school.

Upon graduating from high school, Barbara enrolled in Smith College where, she admits, she was a poor student. She preferred to think about George, who was flying missions in the South Pacific, rather than concentrate on her studies. She wrote him often, but his letters to her arrived irregularly, and usually several came at one time. Of one particular time when Barbara hadn't heard from George in a while, she said,

We heard nothing from him that September, but that was not unusual. Mail was slow. Then one day I got a letter from Doug West, a pilot in George's squadron, who told me George had been shot down. . . . I called Mrs. Bush [George's mother] who had just gotten the same notice. . . . We were frantic . . . I really don't remember the next three days—they are just a blur—but the Navy got a message to the Bushes that George had been picked up and was in Hawaii. . . . His two crew mates, however, had been lost.[76]

On January 6, 1945, Barbara married George Bush. Soon after the wedding, George completed his service time and began his education at Yale. After graduating, George got a job in Odessa, Texas, and the family, which now included their young son, George W., packed up their car and headed west.

Married Life

After World War II ended in 1945, the U.S. economy was growing rapidly. The stronger economy left people with money to buy cars and take driving vacations. As a result, production of oil became very important. When new fields were discovered in west Texas, people came from all over the world to get in on the "black gold" rush, Texas oil. It was oil that would make George Bush a wealthy man.

Life in Odessa was good for the Bushes, and Barbara and George quickly made friends with many other families in the area. Barbara wrote in her *Memoir*, "We had all been uprooted; we all had young children; and we all were having a lot of fun. . . . We all worked in the Little Theater [nationwide organization for amateur actors] and the YMCA. . . . We took turns having cookouts on our tiny patios or in backyards and watching each other's children. When the chips were down, all of us were there for each other."[77] These young married couples made the community and friends their family.

Barbara Pierce married navy lieutenant George Bush in New York on January 6, 1945.

It was at this point that the most tragic chapter of Barbara's life began and soon ended. In early March 1953, while the family was living in Midland, Texas, her three-year-old daughter Robin was diagnosed with leukemia, a disease Barbara and George had never heard of. They rushed the little girl to a hospital in New York where, for the next seven months, Barbara stood by her daughter's bedside as the youngster was given all the latest treatments. All efforts failed, however, and Robin died in October 1953.

Barbara and George were devastated by the loss of their child. They knew, however, that for the sake of their two sons, they had to get back to some sort of normal life. It wasn't easy. Barbara explained, saying, "I wanted to get back to real life, but there is a dance you have to go through to get there. When I wanted to cut out, George made me talk to him, and he shared with me. . . . He made me remember that the loss was not just mine, it was his, Georgie's and Jeb's."[78]

A Memorable Journey

The Bush family ultimately included four sons, George W., Jeb, Neil, and Marvin, and one daughter, Dorothy. It became a tradition for them to travel at least once every other year to Kennebunkport in Maine, where the family rented a house for a month. Typically, Barbara would load the children in a station wagon and drive all the way. In the summer of 1957, Barbara was driving home from Kennebunkport with her children and a young black woman named Otha Fitzgerald, who was hired to help her on the journey. Everything went smoothly until the group reached the South. Fitzgerald was not welcome in any restaurant, hotel, or motel. Insisting that Barbara and the children should eat in the restaurant and get themselves rooms, Fitzgerald said she would eat and sleep in the car. Barbara would not accept those conditions.

The group picnicked at convenience stores and searched until they found a Howard Johnson's Motel in Oklahoma that would accept them all. Barbara said, "I was ashamed of our system that could tell this fine woman she was not equal."[79] From that trip, Barbara learned that there were many aspects of life—particularly the ugliness of racial prejudice—that she had never been aware of. It was an experience that impressed on Barbara the need for changes in a system that would not accept American citizens as paying customers simply because of their skin color.

After several successful years in oil, George talked with Barbara about his desire to enter public service and run for political office. Barbara wholeheartedly supported his decision. George's first of-

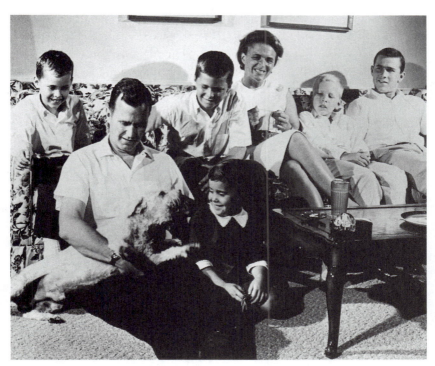

The Bush family at home in Houston, Texas, in 1964.

fice was chairman of the Republican Party of Harris County, Texas. After he was elected to the U.S. House of Representatives in 1966, the family moved again, this time to Washington, D.C.

Barbara immersed herself in the whirl of Washington receptions and luncheons. Janet Steiger, wife of Wisconsin congressman Bill Steiger, met Barbara at one of the gatherings. She said, "By the end of a couple of hours, you knew there was a person you wanted to know better. I think that was pretty much shared by everybody who met her. There was a lot of lively warmth, she seemed so real."[80] Barbara made friends quickly. The first two years flew by, and George was unopposed for reelection in 1968.

George Bush spent most of that year campaigning for Richard M. Nixon's presidential election. After Nixon won, the two remained friends, and in 1970, Nixon offered George the position of ambassador to the United Nations.

The early '70s were a disastrous time for Washington. Only three years after Nixon gave George the job at the United Nations, the president found himself being investigated in connection with a break-in at the Democratic National Committee headquarters in the Watergate Hotel in Washington, D.C. Nixon was accused of being behind the crime. Recalling how she felt at that time, Barbara

Upon her husband's 1966 election to the House of Representatives, Barbara and the family moved again, to Washington, D.C.

said in her *Memoir*, "It got so bad that my childhood friend Milly Dent, whose husband, Fred, was Secretary of Commerce, became my only tennis partner. We couldn't find two others who did not think President Nixon was lying. It was an unpleasant time for everyone."[81] Finally, President Nixon resigned and Vice President Gerald Ford took over. Ford gave Bush his pick of jobs in the new administration.

Surprising everyone, George chose to become chief of the Liaison Office to the Republic of China. He and Barbara lived there for two years before returning to the United States.

First Presidential Campaign

In 1979, after many years of public service, George Bush announced his candidacy for president of the United States. It was during this presidential campaign that Barbara began to consider what her role would be if her husband were elected. One day, while jogging in Houston's Memorial Park, she thought about all the things that worried her: the environment, the homeless, teenage pregnancies, hunger, crime, and more. She realized that being able to read would help everyone get an education and education would solve many of those problems. Literacy would be her cause.

Barbara wrote later in her *Memoir*,

> I felt the subject I chose should help the most people possible, but not cost the government more money and not be

controversial. A president has enough troubles—he does not need a wife to stir up more controversy for him. . . . Finally after much thought, I realized everything I worried about would be better if more people could read and comprehend. More people would stay in school and get an education, meaning fewer people would turn to the streets and get involved with crime or drugs, become pregnant, or lose their homes. It seemed that simple.[82]

Although George failed in his first bid for the presidency, Ronald Reagan, the 1980 Republican presidential nominee, chose him as his running mate. Now the wife of a vice presidential candidate, Barbara traveled all over the nation telling people not only about George Bush but also about Ronald Reagan, whom she barely knew.

Second Lady

When Reagan was elected president, the Bushes moved into the vice presidential mansion, a thirty-three-room Victorian house on the U.S. Naval Observatory grounds in Washington, D.C. As vice

Barbara Bush (left) barely knew Ronald Reagan (second from right) when he chose her husband as his running mate in 1980.

president, her husband was expected to travel over the globe, taking care of the duties the president assigned him. As second lady, Barbara was able to devote time and energy to the country and her cause of literacy.

Like many other wives of politicians, Barbara loved the life but hated the limelight, especially since she liked to drop protocol whenever she could. For instance, traditionally, visiting dignitaries were seated at dinner parties according to position or military rank. Barbara, however, preferred to seat her guests where they would be most comfortable.

During her years as a politician's wife, Barbara tried to keep out of the news unless it concerned literacy, but she wasn't always successful. In fact, she made a major misstep during the 1984 presidential campaign. Walter Mondale, the Democratic nominee running against President Reagan, chose as his running mate Geraldine Ferraro, the first woman ever to be chosen by a major candidate as running mate.

On a campaign trip to New York, Barbara made one of the most outspoken mistakes of her political life. She was in the press section of the plane, visiting with Terry Hunt of the Associated Press and Ira Allen of UPI. The day before, Mondale had baited Reagan, calling George Bush a rich, elitist vice president. The comment made Barbara angry, since she knew from reports that Ms. Ferraro and her husband were worth at least $4 million. When Hunt and Allen began to tease Barbara, she said, "That rich . . . well, it rhymes with rich . . . could buy George Bush any day."[83] It wasn't long before that statement was repeated on every radio and television station nationwide. Barbara was horrified.

The first thing she did was call Geraldine Ferraro and apologize. Then she called George, who had already left New York for another event, to tell him the predicament she had put herself in. In the end, the situation worked out fine. One of George's advisers recommended that Barbara think of Halloween. She said, "So I marched out smiling and said that I had talked to Ms. Ferraro and apologized for calling her a witch and that she had graciously accepted my apology."[84]

Campaigning for the Presidency

Reagan's eight years in office were up in 1988, and the Republican Party put their hopes in George Bush, trusting his record of public service and his wide knowledge of foreign affairs. There was almost no world leader that the Bushes had not visited during their time in the Reagan administration. So if George won, it

Barbara watches as her husband is sworn in as president in January 1989.

would make for a smooth transition of power. There would be no need for introductions.

Barbara was with George during the entire campaign, completely confident that he was the best man for the job. That campaign, however, proved to be very dirty and filled with negative remarks. During one interview with newscaster Dan Rather, for example, George was accused of being involved in illegal activities, accusations that turned out to be unfounded. Instead of a profile of the candidate, the interview turned into a political exposé filled with comments designed to blacken George's reputation. As a result of that interview, Barbara asked George if he would mind if she skipped further meetings and didn't watch the evening news with him. Listening to her husband being attacked by the press was more than she could stand.

Despite the negative comments, George Bush won the 1988 presidential election. On November 9, 1988, Barbara wrote in her diary, "I awakened this morning with the President-elect of the United States of America."[85] Her life as first lady was about to begin.

Under the Gun

The differences between Barbara and former first lady Nancy Reagan were discussed widely in the press. "I hate that," Barbara once stated, "because first of all, I lose on that particular comparison."[86] The nation, however, saw things differently.

To most, Barbara seemed open and down-to-earth, while Nancy Reagan had appeared cold and detached. Barbara welcomed her family with open arms, while the Reagans rarely saw theirs. Barbara's answer about the similarities became her trademark—humor directed at herself. "As you know, we have a lot in common," Barbara said of Mrs. Reagan. "She adores her husband; I adore mine. She fights drugs; I fight illiteracy. She wears a size three . . . so's my leg."[87]

Besides being interested in comparisons between Barbara and Nancy Reagan, many people also wondered how much influence the new first lady would have on her husband's presidency. Those who listened to George's inaugural address thought they had the answer when he mentioned the homeless, the children with nothing, and those who could not free themselves of welfare. Americans immediately detected the hand of Barbara Bush because those were her areas of concern. Later she denied having anything to do with writing the speech but suggested that sometimes, by close association, those kinds of ideas filter from one person to another. When reporters asked her outright whether she influenced the president in his policies, her answers ranged from a shrug to a comment that even an innocent person could influence another. What she did tell them, though, was that if she had something to say to George, she would most certainly say it openly.

As it turned out, Barbara did have quite a bit of influence over the president. It was the Bushes' habit to wake up early, take coffee and juice to bed, and have what amounted to a work session discussing the issues. Barbara said, "We wake up every morning and read three papers and read things aloud. . . . He will say here's an article you ought to read, you'll find this interesting. Here's an article about your friend, or about this issue, or here's something you asked me about. Sometimes vice versa."[88]

A Call to Service

Not long after the inauguration in January 1989, Barbara started work on her own agenda of fighting illiteracy and educating the public about AIDS. Her work in these areas demonstrated a deep concern for the misfortunes of others. For example, she went to Grandma's House, a home for babies and children suffering from AIDS, and as the press trailed her, Barbara picked up a baby, gave it a kiss, and pulled an older child to her, kissing him also. Barbara discussed with the house director the fear that people have about personal contact with those who have AIDS, particularly adults. Later, Barbara turned to a young man who had AIDS and, as the photographers took pictures, gave him a big hug as well. "There is a need for compassion," she said. "You can hug and pick up babies and people who have the AIDS virus." In response, the local director smiled and told reporters, "You can't imagine what one hug from the First Lady is worth."[89]

All her life, Barbara had tried to assist others when they needed her support. As first lady, she used her influence to help even more people and encouraged others to follow her example. Susan Baker, wife of Jim Baker, George Bush's secretary of state, said of Barbara, "She sees needs. She involves herself in them and she gives others the strength and the courage they need to involve themselves."[90]

She took that strength and courage to other groups as well. When the president of the Federation of Parents and Friends of Lesbians and Gays asked her to reach out to the millions of gay Americans and their families, Barbara accepted the invitation. She said, "I firmly believe that we cannot tolerate discrimination against any individuals or groups. . . . I appreciate your sharing the information about your organization and your encouraging me to help change attitudes. . . . [Discrimination] always brings with it pain and perpetuates hate and intolerance."[91]

First Lady Barbara Bush worked tirelessly in her efforts to fight illiteracy.

Wellesley Controversy

Although Barbara was popular, not everyone appreciated her choosing marriage and family ahead of a career. Some graduating seniors at Wellesley College were among those who disputed Barbara's values. When Barbara accepted an invitation to speak to their graduating class in May 1990, several seniors protested the choice of the first lady on the grounds that she had gained her achievements in life only because her husband was president of the United States. Despite the controversy, Barbara refused to cancel her speech. She did not apologize for her position on family and did not complain about her treatment by the student body.

Instead, Barbara used her speech to express her ideas. She said,

> As important as your obligations as a doctor, lawyer, or business leader will be, you are a human being first, and those human connections—with spouses, with children, with friends—are the most important investments you will ever make. At the end of your life, you will never regret not having passed one more test . . . winning one more verdict . . . or one more deal. You will regret time not spent with a husband, a friend, a child, or a parent. [92]

In a commencement speech at Wellesley College in 1990, Barbara Bush stressed the importance of being a successful human being.

Even the career-oriented seniors at Wellesley came to appreciate that Barbara's outlook on family and her pride in being a grandmother did not mean she was not a successful woman.

Even though Barbara felt there was much more she could do in her role as first lady and she was certain her husband was a great leader, she knew it would someday end, although she wasn't ready for the end to come as soon as it did. Although she was disappointed when her husband lost the 1992 presidential election to Bill Clinton, she understood the country's need for change. Americans were worried about unemployment and the nation's economy and felt George Bush was more interested in foreign affairs than problems at home.

Life After the White House

Soon after the election, Barbara began to long for the privacy she had once enjoyed. She craved the comfort of home and family and intended to get back to a normal life as quickly as possible. To do so would mean easing back into anonymity at home in Houston. That never happened. There were so many tourists around the Bushes' home hoping to get a glimpse of the former president and first lady that the Texas legislature passed a law allowing the Bushes to gate their street.

The gate kept people away from Barbara's home but couldn't prevent them from approaching her in public. Barbara's admirers followed her everywhere. At stores, they often stopped her and asked, "Are you Barbara Bush?" "No," she'd say, "she's much older than I am," or "No, but I'm mistaken for her all the time."[93] Using humor was the only way Barbara could think of to get on with her life without being rude to the people who followed her continuously.

When George retired, Barbara had believed she was out of politics for good. However, two of her sons ran for governor of their states and won: Jeb in Florida and George W. in Texas. And when the 2000 presidential campaign began, George W. announced his candidacy. He asked his mother to speak for him at a rally in 1999, and she happily agreed. The speech went well, and the welcoming reception she received proved that Americans still loved Barbara Bush.

CHAPTER 6

Hillary Rodham Clinton: Presidential Partner

Bill Clinton's admiration for his wife's talents is so great that, during the 1992 presidential campaign, he promised the nation they would be getting "two leaders dedicated to America's future for the price of one."[94] He made it clear that Hillary was a key part of his political life and would serve essentially as his partner.

Just as he depended heavily on her political skill throughout the campaign, as president he continued to turn to her as a trusted adviser. A close Clinton aide said, "A speech to write, 'Get Hillary.' A speech needs a rewrite, 'Get Hillary.' The President has a problem he wants to chew over, 'Get Hillary.' The point is you never go wrong in getting Hillary."[95]

As critics battered her husband with allegations of indiscretions, Hillary stood by his side, demonstrating her loyalty to him and his future. She publicly showed with a smile or a touch that they were still partners. Donnie Radcliffe's book said it best: "Throughout the successes and scandals of the Clinton presidency, Hillary emerged the way she had begun: as a woman of substance, courage, and vision—a leader in her own right."[96]

The Early Years

Hillary Diane Rodham was born on October 26, 1947, in Chicago, and grew up in Park Ridge, Illinois. Dorothy Howell Rodham, her mother, and Hugh Rodham, her father, expected only the best from Hillary and her two younger brothers. When Hillary couldn't play baseball as well as other girls, they coached her. Although her grades in school were good, her parents required excellence. Their expectations forced Hillary to reach deep within herself and learn her own potential. She said, "I never felt anything but support from my family. Whatever I thought I could do and be, they supported. There was no distinction between me and my brothers or any barriers thrown up to me . . . because I was a girl."[97]

In 1965, Hillary graduated from high school with honors, in the top 5 percent of her class, and with a stunning list of achievements. A high school classmate said, "Hillary was so take charge, so determined, so involved in every single activity."[98] She could attend any college she wanted. Ultimately, she chose Wellesley College near Boston, Massachusetts.

A Changing World

At Wellesley Hillary was exposed to political activism. The late 1960s were a time of tremendous social change in the United States. Young women particularly were questioning their role in society; many believed they had been undervalued and discouraged from achieving their own goals. Instead of being accepted for their individual qualities, women charged that men

Hillary Diane Rodham Clinton was her husband's most trusted adviser throughout his two terms in office.

cared only about how beautiful a woman was. In protest, Hillary and many others across the country began to dress simply and discarded makeup and elaborate hairstyles. Also, whereas marriage had once been women's only choice in life, many women now decided they would choose for themselves whether to marry and have children or to pursue a career.

Of that time, Hillary once said, "Both the college and the country were going through a period of rapid, sometimes tumultuous changes. . . . My classmates and I felt challenged."[99] Ultimately, it was through politics that Hillary decided to meet those challenges.

During her college years, Hillary's parental training guided her. Hillary had grown up in a home where current events and politics were discussed at the dinner table; her father maintained a strong Republicanism and her mother took the Democratic side. The Rodhams believed that politics could solve the problems facing the world, so for Hillary, politics became a means to achieve

Hillary Rodham graduated in 1965 from Maine Township South High School in Park Ridge, Illinois, in the top 5 percent of her class.

major and necessary changes. Wellesley president Ruth Adams said of Hillary, "She was . . . interested in affecting change, but from within rather than outside the system. . . . [She] wanted to go to law school . . . and change from within."[100]

Law School

Before she could leave for law school, however, Hillary had to graduate from Wellesley. During her senior year, she became very interested in community programs designed to help the underprivileged. She decided that her thesis should focus on whether these programs that attempted to fight poverty were effective. She spent a year studying them and discovered that, while they were constructive, they were not enough. She wrote, "Organizing the poor for community actions [programs] to improve their own lives may have in certain circumstances, short-term benefits for the poor but would never solve their major problems. You need much more than that. You need leadership, programs, [and] constitutional doctrines."[101]

Hillary was determined to use the law to accomplish these things. Although she entertained the idea of attending the prestigious Harvard Law School, in the end she decided on Yale.

During her years at Yale Law School, Hillary developed a deep interest in child welfare issues. She spent one summer as an intern with Marian Edelman, a civil rights lawyer who was committed to using her Yale education to benefit poor children. At Edelman's request, Hillary concentrated on the problems facing the children of migrant workers. She met families who lived in shacks, parents who couldn't afford medicine for their children, and adolescents who had to work in the fields instead of going to school. She agreed with Edelman, who said, "Children are the unrecognized, neglected and mistreated minority in America. . . . Children's rights may well provide the most promising vehicle for addressing the broader problems of poverty and race."[102]

The summer proved to be a turning point for Hillary. She went back to school in the fall with a growing commitment toward children. Hillary's lifetime of working for the rights of children and the poor women who most often faced caring for them grew from that experience.

Meeting Bill Clinton

It was just after the summer with Edelman that Hillary first met William Jefferson Clinton, also a student at Yale. The tall, handsome Clinton was very charming, and he entertained Yale students with colorful tales of his beloved Arkansas. Bill and Hillary ran into each other often, but it was Hillary who grew tired of Clinton staring at her in the law library and finally initiated an introduction. Bill's looks, his cool self-assurance, and his obvious intelligence were attractive to Hillary. She once said that in her first conversation with him, she was struck "by how he was able to be so smart and so human, at the same time. I just had never met anybody like that. . . . Bill was just extraordinary in his interest in other people. His commitment to policies and the public interest just stood out."[103]

Their mutual fascination with law and politics drew them together as much as their attraction to each other. Friends at Yale said their personalities were perfectly suited, but at first their families did not agree. Bill's mother was appalled by Hillary's homely dress, unkempt hair, and unshaven legs, attributes that were common to feminists of the '70s. Bill responded by telling his mother, "Look, I want you to know that I've had it up to here with beauty queens. I have to have somebody I can talk to."[104] Hillary's parents also complained, mostly about the couple's obsession with political discussions; they talked of nothing but Arkansas and politics. The Rodhams, too, however, ultimately accepted the relationship.

In 1971, the couple rented a three-room apartment where they lived together and entertained friends with lively debates. Both continued law school and were active in political campaigns together. Bill was captivated by Hillary, and she appreciated Bill's political potential. There were problems, though, the most important of which were their differences in personality. Bill was committed to political life in Arkansas, while Hillary was much more interested in national issues. Much later, Hillary spoke of those days before they married, saying, "We were both very concerned about our country and its direction and fascinated by politics and commitment to public service. . . . We also realized that a marriage between two people like us was never, ever going to be easy, if it could happen at all. When we graduated from law school he went right back to Arkansas. I wanted nothing to do with that."[105]

Investigating Richard Nixon

Following her graduation from Yale, Hillary moved to Washington, D.C., because it was from there she believed the momentous decisions affecting the nation would be made. In 1973, Hillary had the opportunity to be closely involved with Washington politics. That fall, John Doar, the man chosen by the House Judiciary Committee to investigate President Richard Nixon's involvement in a break-in at the Democratic National Committee offices in Washington, D.C.'s Watergate Hotel, hired Hillary to work on the investigating committee. Hillary called that opportunity "one of the greatest experiences professionally and politically that I've ever had, to be in-

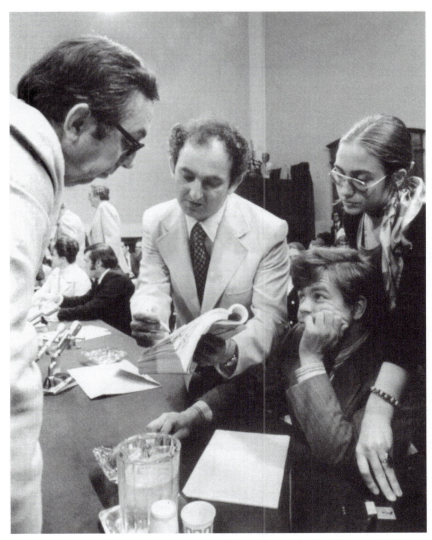

Hillary (top right) was an essential member of the House Judiciary Committee's Watergate investigation.

volved with lawyers of that caliber and that level of commitment to the country. What a gift! I was twenty-six years old."[106]

Hillary was intelligent and a hard worker. As a result, she quickly became essential to Doar's investigation and a member of his inner circle of trusted workers. In fact, she was so important to him that when she took a brief vacation, Doar summoned her to Washington, offering to send a plane to bring her back. He had come to rely that much on Hillary's abilities.

On August 9, 1974, Hillary's time with the committee ended when President Nixon resigned due to the evidence against him.

Hillary said Nixon's resignation was a great relief to her, and she felt it was also a resounding victory for the system. The fact that the United States could face the resignation of a leader without incident or turmoil was proof that the government performed as it was supposed to.

The end of the investigation also put Hillary out of a job and Bill urged her to come to Arkansas. "What was I to do?" she said. "I could have gone to work for a big law firm in a place like Chicago. . . . I could have gone back to work for the Children's Defense Fund, stayed on that career path. . . . I also knew I had to deal with a whole other side of life—the emotional side, where we live and where we grow and when it is all said and done, where the most important parts of life take place."[107] In the end, she decided to move to Arkansas to be with Bill.

Arkansas

In Fayetteville, Hillary took a teaching position at the University of Arkansas, where Bill was already at work. She taught criminal law and criminal procedure, and her students acknowledged that she was a demanding teacher. Despite living and working with Bill, Hillary had not yet made up her mind about marriage. At that point, her career options looked limitless and she worried that marriage would tie her to Arkansas and Bill's future, not her own. Bill made no secret of the fact that he was committed to politics in Arkansas.

Matters came to a head after a trip to see her family in Park Ridge. Hillary had gone away to clear her mind and consider her options. She came back to Fayetteville to find that Bill had bought a house she had admired. He hoped his gesture would touch her heart and sway her to marry him. She finally agreed, and on Saturday, October 11, 1975, just before Hillary was twenty-eight, they were married. Bill was poised to run for attorney general of Arkansas, and Hillary played a vital role in his campaign. She helped make decisions on policy and about whom to hire. Bill trusted her judgment and depended on her suggestions. Bill won the office of attorney general, and Hillary went to work for the Rose Law Firm in Little Rock, Arkansas. A year later, in 1978, her husband was elected governor of the state, and Hillary moved into the governor's mansion.

During Bill's governorship, an office he won five times, the Clintons had a daughter, whom they named Chelsea Victoria. Hillary became well known for her work around the state, particularly regarding education. After Clinton was elected to a second term, he concluded that the education system in the state of Arkansas was outdated and needed to be revamped. He chose Hillary to head the group that would study the issue and make recommendations. After touring Arkansas, Hillary instituted a program called Home Instruction for Preschool Youths, or HIPY. It was a program that went into rural Arkansas homes and worked with the families to get children off to a good start in school.

Presidential Partner

In 1992, Bill Clinton officially announced his candidacy for president. Hillary would in effect act as his chief adviser. George Stephanopoulos, who was one of Bill's campaign managers, spoke of Hillary as being in on every important conversation, analyzing the election, and outlining the work that needed to be done. Bill Clinton still trusted his wife's talent and her intellect. After winning the election, one of his first acts was to appoint Hillary head of his Task Force on National Health Care Reform.

Hillary, pictured here at a rally for her husband, was involved in every aspect of the presidential campaign.

The new president knew that the country's health care system needed an overhaul because it failed to meet the needs of children and those who were uninsured. When Hillary began to analyze the situation and discuss possible remedies, she found that the problem was much more complicated than she first believed. The major obstacle concerned the number of people who did not want a new health care system. She said her biggest problem was "overcoming . . . the extraordinary power of people who want to keep things as they are . . . this . . . blockade against reality and all these people who basically think things are fine."[108]

Hillary called her attempt at revamping the health care system the hardest thing she'd ever tried to do, especially since many people who had a difference of opinion concerning the health care issue or her husband's administration took aim at Hillary. Enemies of the Clintons called her abrasive, a liar, and a radical feminist.

In September 1994, Congress rejected Hillary's recommendations for revitalizing health care, saying they were too broad and unworkable. All her effort had been wasted, and she felt disappointed but not destroyed. Confident in her own abilities, she was determined to go on. She once said, "Excellence is not found in any single moment of our lives. It is not about those who shine always in the sun or those who fail to succeed in the darkness of human error or mistake, it is about who we are, what we believe in, what we do with every day of our lives."[109]

Hillary knew herself and her options. She intended to reach her goals and to earn the public's respect. Her first step in

First Lady Hillary Clinton was appointed by her husband to head his Task Force of National Health Care Reform.

doing so was to retreat and decide what her next step should be. Hillary wanted to be certain that anything she organized or stood for in the future would be acceptable to the American public. After a few months of self-evaluation, Hillary returned to the public arena and took a highly visible stance on women's and children's rights that commanded the world's attention.

Championing Women's Rights

The United Nations held its Fourth World Conference on Women in Beijing, China, in September 1995. Hillary decided to attend as honorary leader of the group, even though U.N. ambassador Madeleine Albright would act as chairperson of the American delegation. It was a time of strain between the United States and China because of an incident six years earlier on June 5, 1989,

Hillary Clinton used her high-profile and powerful position as First Lady to call for women's rights to be recognized worldwide.

when the Chinese government ordered Beijing student protesters shot or jailed. Presidential advisers in Washington were worried that Hillary's trip might worsen the already tense relations if she directly attacked China's human rights issues at the conference. On the other hand, Chinese officials wanted Hillary to attend, hoping her presence might be a signal that the United States wanted to improve relations. Hillary delighted both sides. Without mentioning China or any other country specifically, she listed abuses suffered by women all over the world. She concluded by saying, "If there is one message that echoes far from this conference, it is that human rights are women's rights . . . and women's rights are human rights."[110] Hillary's image improved worldwide.

When her husband won a second presidential term in 1996, Hillary prepared an international tour in support of women's rights. In March 1997, she began a two-week visit to African nations to meet with women leaders. Hillary's speech in Kampala, Uganda, set the tone for her work over the next three years. After pointing out that women make up more than half of the world's population, she called for women's rights to be recognized worldwide. She said,

> Women will not flourish and neither will democracy if women continue to be undervalued inside and outside the home. I'm often told by economists . . . that the work women do does not count. When I think of the gathering of wood, fetching water, raising children, doctoring family members, keeping communities together, I often think to myself, if women stopped working inside and outside the home tomorrow, the economy of the world would stop working. . . . Women must be assured the respect their work deserves . . . they must be assured the opportunity to earn a decent income and be economically self-sufficient. When women are able to contribute to their own economic self-sufficiency, their husbands and children prosper, and their communities prosper as well.[111]

For these efforts, Hillary earned worldwide support. In May of 1998, in Geneva, Switzerland, she was awarded a $40,000 prize for her work on behalf of women and children. The money was donated by the United Arab Emirates and was awarded through the World Health Organization. Hillary gave the money to a charity devoted to reducing infant death.

Just a year or so earlier when asked about how to survive a life in politics, she had answered, "The best way to escape the politics of one's time is to totally withdraw. Perhaps put a bag over your head and somehow make it clear that you have no opinions and no ideas about anything."[112] Her actions made it perfectly clear that Hillary Rodham Clinton had changed her mind. She had chosen women's rights as her cause and pursued it with courage and diligence. Hillary championed rights for women who had been mistreated and humiliated.

The Monica Lewinsky Affair

Life for Hillary didn't always go so smoothly. In January 1998, the United States and the world learned that Bill Clinton had been having an affair with White House intern Monica Lewinsky and lied about it. Hillary defended her husband when she heard the accusations. It wasn't until the end that she realized her husband had lied to her as well as the nation.

Hillary stood by her husband during the dark days of scandal. The Clintons are pictured here attending a dinner on the second day of his impeachment trial.

Those around Hillary said that, although she was angry and hurt, she remained professional, even offering her talents as a lawyer and political adviser to her husband. Reverend Jesse Jackson, a Clinton family friend, maintained that even as the drama was building, Hillary was organizing Bill's testimony.

When it was certain that Bill would be impeached, Hillary insisted on being kept informed of the proceedings. One aide said, "She gets a briefing book [notes on the day's activities] every night . . . and she reads it. . . . The worse things get, the more focused she becomes."[113]

The American people responded to Hillary's situation with sympathy. They opened their hearts to her and also to the Clinton's daughter, Chelsea. It was as if, because of the crisis, people identified with her as never before. When she remained steadfastly beside her husband after being so publicly embarrassed, she gained many people's respect. While a minority cried out for her to abandon her husband, others admired the strength she showed by standing with him under extremely trying circumstances.

When her husband was acquitted in February of 1999, Hillary's approval rate was at 68 percent. Putting the Lewinsky affair behind her, Hillary continued her quest for women's rights. She told the Senior Executive Women's Forum in Chicago in October 1999 that even though American women face hardships at times, it doesn't compare with problems facing women in other countries. She called women in the States blessed and said, "And as with any blessing, it carries an obligation. What will we do to make sure our voices are heard? . . . Women who don't have any position from which to speak—women who don't have a voice that will be heard—need our voices. Politics is about organizing and raising those voices here at home and around the world."[114]

Hillary's popularity remained high, and many avenues of opportunity opened as her husband's presidency came to an end. Early in 2000, Hillary announced her candidacy for senator in the state of New York. She quickly purchased a home there and began campaigning. Constituents were divided almost evenly about her campaign, and Hillary accepted that as a challenge. She threw herself wholeheartedly into the process, determined to make herself heard.

As she always had, Hillary trusted in the power of the political process. She expressed this view in 1992 in a speech at her old high school:

I firmly believe that the whole purpose of politics—and it's not just elective politics on a presidential or gubernatorial

Hillary waves to the audience at Purchase College, State University of New York moments before announcing her candidacy for the New York Senate in February 2000.

level but politics with a small p [local politics]—is how people get together, how they agree on their goals, how they move together to realize those goals, how they make the absolutely inevitable [unavoidable] tradeoffs between deeply held beliefs that are incompatible.[115]

When *Newsweek* magazine ran an exclusive article in June 2000 about the possibility of a woman becoming president of the United States, Hillary Rodham Clinton's name was at the top of the list. Hillary immediately defused comments that she would run for president in 2004, saying that if she were elected to the Senate, she would serve her full term of six years. (She did not rule out a presidential bid in 2008, however.) Whatever the future holds, though, Hillary Rodham Clinton is determined to conquer it just as she did the obstacles she encountered in her eight years as first lady.

NOTES

Introduction: A Changing Role

1. Quoted in C. David Heymann, *A Woman Named Jackie*. New York: Carol Communications, 1989, pp. 348–49.

2. Quoted in Edith P. Mayo, ed., *The Smithsonian Book of the First Ladies: Their Lives, Times, and Issues*. New York: Henry Holt, 1996, p. 34.

Chapter 1: Sarah Childress Polk

3. Quoted in Carl S. Anthony, *First Ladies: The Saga of the Presidents' Wives and Their Power*, vol. 1. New York: William Morrow, 1990, p. 35.

4. Quoted in Paul F. Boller Jr., *Presidential Wives: An Anecdotal History*. New York: Oxford University Press, 1998, p. 89.

5. Quoted in Anthony, *First Ladies*, vol. 1, p. 137.

6. Quoted in Boller, *Presidential Wives*, p. 89.

7. Quoted in Anthony, *First Ladies*, vol. 1, p. 138.

8. Quoted in Anthony, *First Ladies*, vol. 1, p. 138.

9. Quoted in Anthony, *First Ladies*, vol. 1, p. 139.

10. Quoted in Boller, *Presidential Wives*, p. 94.

11. Quoted in Anthony, *First Ladies*, vol. 1, p. 141.

12. Quoted in Anthony, *First Ladies*, vol. 1, p. 142.

13. Quoted in Anthony, *First Ladies*, vol. 1, p. 140.

Chapter 2: Eleanor Roosevelt Roosevelt

14. Quoted in Russell Freedman, *Eleanor Roosevelt: A Life of Discovery*. New York: Clarion, 1993, p. 168.

15. Quoted in Anthony, *First Ladies*, vol. 1, p. 27.

16. Quoted in Freedman, *Eleanor Roosevelt*, pp. 50–51.

17. Quoted in Freedman, *Eleanor Roosevelt*, p. 55.

18. Joseph P. Lash, *Eleanor and Franklin*. Garden City, NY: Doubleday, 1971, p. 358.

19. Quoted in Joseph P. Lash, *Love, Eleanor: Eleanor and Her Friends*. Garden City, NY: Doubleday, 1982, pp. 71–72.

20. Quoted in Lash, *Love, Eleanor*, p. 80.

21. Quoted in Freedman, *Eleanor Roosevelt*, p. 74.

22. Quoted in Lash, *Love, Eleanor*, p. 80.

23. Quoted in Freedman, *Eleanor Roosevelt*, pp. 92–93.

24. Quoted in Freedman, *Eleanor Roosevelt*, p. 100.

25. Quoted in Anthony, *First Ladies*, vol. 1, p. 455.

26. Quoted in Freedman, *Eleanor Roosevelt*, p. 131.

27. Quoted in Anthony, *First Ladies*, vol. 1, p. 498.

28. Quoted in Freedman, *Eleanor Roosevelt*, p. 142.

29. Quoted in Freedman, *Eleanor Roosevelt*, p. 165.

30. Quoted in Freedman, *Eleanor Roosevelt*, p. 77.

Chapter 3: Jacqueline Bouvier Kennedy

31. Quoted in Boller, *Presidential Wives*, p. 364.

32. Quoted in Boller, *Presidential Wives*, p. 355.

33. Quoted in Boller, *Presidential Wives*, p. 361.

34. Quoted in Heymann, *A Woman Named Jackie*, p. 208.

35. Quoted in Kitty Kelley, *Jackie Oh!* New York: Ballantine Books, 1978, p. 47.

36. Quoted in Heymann, *A Woman Named Jackie*, p. 218.

37. Quoted in Heymann, *A Woman Named Jackie*, p. 220.

38. Quoted in Heymann, *A Woman Named Jackie*, p. 266.

39. Quoted in Carl S. Anthony, *First Ladies: The Saga of the Presidents' Wives and Their Power*, vol. 2. New York: William Morrow, 1991, p. 27.

40. Quoted in Kelley, *Jackie Oh!* p. 168.

41. Quoted in Anthony, *First Ladies*, vol. 2, p. 75.

42. Quoted in Deborah Shapley, *Promise and Power*. Boston: Little, Brown, 1993, pp. 174–75.

43. Quoted in Heymann, *A Woman Named Jackie*, p. 349.

44. Quoted in Heymann, *A Woman Named Jackie*, p. 349.

45. Quoted in Anthony, *First Ladies*, vol. 2, p. 94.

46. Quoted in Anthony, *First Ladies*, vol. 2, pp. 98, 99.

47. Mary Barelli Gallagher, *My Life with Jacqueline Kennedy*. New York: Paperback Library, 1970, p. 325.

48. Quoted in Heymann, *A Woman Named Jackie*, p. 408.

49. Quoted in Heymann, *A Woman Named Jackie*, p. 483.

50. Quoted in Boller, *Presidential Wives*, p. 369.

Chapter 4: Betty Bloomer Ford

51. Quoted in "A Dozen Who Made a Difference," *Time*, January 5, 1976, pp. 19–22.

52. Betty Ford, with Chris Chase, *The Times of My Life*. New York: Ballantine Books, 1979, p. 45.

53. Quoted in Ford, *The Times of My Life*, p. 139.

54. Quoted in Ford, *The Times of My Life*, p. 135.

55. Ford, *The Times of My Life*, p. 160.

56. Quoted in *Time*, "Have a Helluva Good Time," July 28, 1975, pp. 10–13.

57. Quoted in Anthony, *First Ladies*, vol. 2, pp. 223–24.

58. Quoted in Anthony, *First Ladies*, vol. 2, p. 222.

59. Quoted in Boller, *Presidential Wives*, p. 418.

60. Quoted in Boller, *Presidential Wives*, p. 425.

61. Quoted in "Have a Helluva Good Time," pp. 10–13.

62. Quoted in Boller, *Presidential Wives*, p. 425.

63. Quoted in Boller, *Presidential Wives*, p. 426.

64. Quoted in Sheila Rabb Weidenfeld, *First Lady's Lady*. New York: G. P. Putnam's Sons, 1979, p. 146.

65. Quoted in Weidenfeld, *First Lady's Lady*, p. 275.

66. Quoted in Boller, *Presidential Wives*, p. 427.

67. Ford, *The Times of My Life*, p. 281.

68. Weidenfeld, *First Lady's Lady*, p. 372.

69. Ford, *The Times of My Life*, p. 296.

70. Betty Ford, with Chris Chase, *Betty: A Glad Awakening*. New York: Jove Books, 1978, p. 27.

71. Ford, *Betty*, p. xv.

72. Quoted in Anthony, *First Ladies*, vol. 2, p. 224.

Chapter 5: Barbara Pierce Bush

73. Quoted in Donnie Radcliffe, *Simply Barbara Bush: A Portrait of America's Candid First Lady*. New York: Warner Books, 1989, p. 1.

74. Barbara Bush, *Barbara Bush: A Memoir*. New York: St. Martin's Paperbacks, 1994, p. 10.

75. Bush, *A Memoir*, p. 17.

76. Bush, *A Memoir*, p. 23.

77. Bush, *A Memoir*, p. 40.

78. Bush, *A Memoir*, p. 50.

79. Bush, *A Memoir*, pp. 54–55.

80. Quoted in Radcliffe, *Simply Barbara Bush*, pp. 149–50.

81. Bush, *A Memoir*, p. 109.

82. Bush, *A Memoir*, p. 155.

83. Bush, *A Memoir*, p. 208.

84. Bush, *A Memoir*, pp. 208–209.

85. Bush, *A Memoir*, p. 263.

86. Quoted in Radcliffe, *Simply Barbara Bush*, p. 14.

87. Quoted in Radcliffe, *Simply Barbara Bush*, p. 4.

88. Quoted in Radcliffe, *Simply Barbara Bush*, p. 202.

89. Quoted in Anthony, *First Ladies*, vol. 2, p. 430.

90. Quoted in Anthony, *First Ladies*, vol. 2, p. 429.

91. Quoted in Anthony, *First Ladies*, vol. 2, p. 431.

92. Bush, *A Memoir*, p. 570.

93. Bush, *A Memoir*, pp. 546, 547.

Chapter 6: Hillary Rodham Clinton

94. Quoted in Boller, *Presidential Wives*, p. 483.

95. Quoted in Boller, *Presidential Wives*, p. 483.

96. Donnie Radcliffe, *Hillary Rodham Clinton: The Evolution of a First Lady*. New York: Warner Books, 1999, back cover.

97. Quoted in Donnie Radcliffe, *Hillary Rodham Clinton: A First Lady for Our Time*. New York: Warner Books, 1993, p. 35.

98. Quoted in Joyce Milton, *The First Partner: Hillary Rodham Clinton*. New York: William Morrow, 1999, p. 19.

99. Quoted in Radcliffe, *The Evolution of a First Lady*, p. 57.

100. Quoted in Milton, *The First Partner*, p. 28.

101. Quoted in Radcliffe, *The Evolution of a First Lady*, p. 77.

102. Quoted in Milton, *The First Partner*, p. 44.

103. Quoted in Radcliffe, *The Evolution of a First Lady*, p. 101.

104. Quoted in Virginia Clinton Kelley, with James Morgan, *Leading with My Heart*. New York: Pocket Books, 1994, p. 203.

105. Quoted in Radcliffe, *A First Lady for Our Time*, p. 118.

106. Quoted in Radcliffe, *A First Lady for Our Time*, p. 120.

107. Quoted in Radcliffe, *The Evolution of a First Lady*, p. 130.

108. Quoted in Radcliffe, *The Evolution of a First Lady*, p. 252.

109. Quoted in Radcliffe, *The Evolution of a First Lady*, p. 242.

110. Quoted in Milton, *The First Partner*, p. 353.

111. Speech at the Nile Conference Center, Kampala, Uganda, March 28, 1997.

112. Quoted in Milton, *The First Partner*, p. 375.

113. Quoted in Radcliffe, *The Evolution of a First Lady*, pp. 320–21.

114. Speech at the Senior Executive Women's Forum, Chicago, Illinois, October 26, 1999.

115. Quoted in Radcliffe, *The Evolution of a First Lady*, p. 24.

FOR FURTHER READING

Liz Carpenter, *Ruffles and Flourishes*. New York: Doubleday, 1970. This is a lighthearted story of various first ladies.

Beatrice Gormley, *First Ladies: Women Who Called the White House Home*. New York: Scholastic, 1997. Concise profiles and photos of each first lady.

Edith P. Mayo, ed., *The Smithsonian Book of the First Ladies: Their Lives, Times, and Issues*. New York: Henry Holt, 1996. Beautifully illustrated, with historical notes. Special sections are devoted to other famous women of the times.

Margaret Truman, *First Ladies*. New York: Fawcett Columbine, 1995. A genial profile of first ladies from the viewpoint of someone who had lived in the White House herself. Interesting and informative, it compares the women who were first ladies in a way no one else has done.

WORKS CONSULTED

Books

Carl S. Anthony, *First Ladies: The Saga of the Presidents' Wives and Their Power*. Vols. 1 and 2. New York: William Morrow, 1990 and 1991. Both these volumes are in-depth studies of the ladies who lived in the White House. Anthony interweaves the stories rather than stacking them one over the other, showing how the first ladies' lives flowed together. He also chronicles the sisterhood that was felt among these women and how they attempted to aid one another.

Paul F. Boller Jr., *Presidential Wives: An Anecdotal History*. New York: Oxford University Press, 1998. This book is filled with interesting points about the ladies during their lives. Boller's scholarly work is easy to read and very interesting. Its format is designed for easy reference.

Barbara Bush, *Barbara Bush: A Memoir*. New York: St. Martin's Paperbacks, 1994. Barbara's day-to-day life, almost in diary format. Easy to read, with her own wit thrown in to make it more enjoyable, this book reveals a lady who is a mother first and a "best" friend to thousands.

Betty Ford, with Chris Chase, *Betty: A Glad Awakening*. New York: Jove Books, 1978. This inspiring story of Betty's recovery from addiction is very warm and personal. Written with the help of her family and friends, this book provides an accurate account of Betty's spirit and courage.

Betty Ford, with Chris Chase, *The Times of My Life*. New York: Ballantine Books, 1979. This book is an almanac with an overview of Betty's family and personal life.

Russell Freedman, *Eleanor Roosevelt: A Life of Discovery*. New York: Clarion, 1993. Freedman's writing is fast paced and covers Eleanor's life quickly and accurately. Without amassing detail, Freedman enables readers to know the real Eleanor, from her almost introverted childhood as an orphan to a public life of serving in the welfare of those less fortunate.

Mary Barelli Gallagher, *My Life with Jacqueline Kennedy*. New York: Paperback Library, 1970. This book deals with Gallagher's life more than Jackie's. It gives a nice view of Jackie's life from the viewpoint of an admirer who worked closely with her for years.

C. David Heymann, *A Woman Named Jackie*. New York: Carol Communications, 1989. An intimate look at Jackie's public life through the eyes of those who knew her best. In-depth interviews deliver a powerful picture of this former first lady.

Kitty Kelley, *Jackie Oh!* New York: Ballantine Books, 1978. Kelley describes a Jackie few people ever knew about.

Virginia Clinton Kelley, with James Morgan, *Leading with My Heart*. New York: Pocket Books, 1994. This book is about Bill Clinton's mother's life. An understanding of Mrs. Kelley's personality and flair builds a more complete picture of her son, President Clinton. She was an independent woman who worked hard and cared for her family, sometimes alone.

Joseph P. Lash, *Eleanor and Franklin*. Garden City, NY: Doubleday, 1971. Lash was a close friend of Eleanor. This work, written soon after her death, it is a warm look at Eleanor's life, with a discussion about the Lucy Mercer affair.

————, *Love, Eleanor: Eleanor and Her Friends*. Garden City, NY: Doubleday, 1982. Here, Lash chronicles Eleanor's life in detail. His access to her personal letters, as well as his being one of her favorite people, contribute to a comprehensive view of her life.

————, *A World of Love*. Garden City, NY: Doubleday, 1984. Lash used all of Eleanor's letters to build this biography of her. It is extremely detailed, with extensive quotations from her own correspondence.

Joyce Milton, *The First Partner: Hillary Rodham Clinton*. New York: William Morrow, 1999. A look at the negative side of Hillary and Bill Clinton's business as well as their life. Milton paints a grim view of Hillary's methods from high school through her years at the Rose Law Firm and in the Arkansas governor's mansion.

Donnie Radcliffe, *Hillary Rodham Clinton: The Evolution of a First Lady*. New York: Warner Books, 1999. Radcliffe writes informative books that are well-rounded with hundreds of comments from multiple sources, providing an unusually comprehensive portrait of her subjects. This is a rewrite of *A First Lady for Our Time* with additional notes on the Monica Lewinsky affair and President Clinton's impeachment.

Donnie Radcliffe, *Hillary Rodham Clinton: A First Lady for Our Time*. New York: Warner Books, 1993. Written soon after Hillary became first lady, this is a warm account of her life before her husband was elected president. Its theme is positive and built on hundreds of interviews of people who knew Hillary Rodham.

Donnie Radcliffe, *Simply Barbara Bush: A Portrait of America's Candid First Lady*. New York: Warner Books, 1989. Written as soon as Barbara became first lady, this book captures the warmth and fun of Barbara Bush and is entertaining and informative.

Deborah Shapley, *Promise and Power*. Boston: Little, Brown, 1993. Shapley's biography of John F. Kennedy's secretary of defense Robert McNamara is a candid portrait of this powerful political figure.

Sheila Rabb Weidenfeld, *First Lady's Lady*. New York: G. P. Putnam's Sons, 1979. Weidenfeld's book is a diary of Betty Ford's days in the White House.

Periodicals

Time, "A Dozen Who Made a Difference," January 5, 1976.

Time, "Have a Helluva Good Time," July 28, 1975.

Website

First Lady's Homepage, *Speeches: 1997–2000*. www.whitehouse.gov.

INDEX

PICTURE CREDITS

ABOUT THE AUTHOR

Sherri Peel Taylor lives with her husband Jerry on the edge of the Kisatchie National Forest near the banks of the Saline Bayou in scenic northern Louisiana. Mrs. Taylor is a "retired" news editor who frequently serves as a freelance feature writer for local newspapers. Some of her work has appeared in *Bowhunter's World*, *North Louisiana Style*, and *Accent on Living* magazines. Her free time is spent with her five granddaughters and in volunteer work.

DATE DUE